It's Not About Size

It's Not About Size

Bigger Brands for Smaller Businesses

Paul Dickinson
with Jonathan Shipp

Virgin

First published in Great Britain in 2001 by
Virgin Publishing Ltd
Thames Wharf Studios
Rainville Road
London
W6 9HA

Extract from *New Mutualism, The Third Way* by Peter Kellner printed courtesy
of The Co-operative Party.

Series Consultant: Professor David Storey
Joint Series Editors: Robert Craven, Grier Palmer

Series design by Janice Mather at Ben Cracknell Studios
Typeset by Phoenix Photosetting, Chatham, Kent
Printed and bound in Great Britain by Mackays of Chatham, Chatham, Kent

Contents

Acknowledgements

I want to extend hearty thanks to a large number of colleagues who have helped prepare and review this book. Foremost is Jonny Shipp, who has been my business partner for more than five years, and who originated many of the theses promulgated here. I would also like to thank all my colleagues at Rufus Leonard, and in particular the great guru of brand development, Steve Howell.

Tessa Tennant was kind enough to offer the better ideas that follow, and some comments about the role of business are copied from her public speeches. Yolanda van den Steen has also been a helpful contributor. Thanks also to numerous other colleagues and clients who have taught me over the years.

Foreword
by Sir Richard Branson

It feels a bit odd to be writing a foreword to a business book. Perhaps it's because I haven't always done business by the book myself. Sometimes I've regretted that, and sometimes I've been glad that I followed my instincts instead of doing what conventional advisers might have recommended.

One thing I've learned is that there's no right way to do things in life. There is no 'magic bullet' for success in business. What works for Virgin Atlantic might not be right for British Airways; what suits your business could be completely wrong for someone else's. But any advice that can help you beat the odds and succeed in business has got to be a good thing. Listening to lots of people's ideas before taking a decision has always been something I have strongly believed in.

Every book in this series has been written by an expert in his or her field, and they've come up with lots of interesting and thought-provoking ideas. But the most important thing is to do what you personally feel is right.

Business should be fun. Enjoy what you do, and success comes within reach.

Good luck!

In shaping economic development in both developed and less-developed countries, brands can seem even more influential than the most powerful politicians. Certainly more people throughout the world will have heard of Coca-Cola than have heard of George W Bush – or even Bill Clinton. Indeed, it may well be that the reason you picked up this book is because of the power of the Virgin brand!

So, if you are running a small business, what do you do when the cards seem so stacked in favour of the big brand? Well, the first thing is to ask yourself what you can learn from observing what big brands do and, when you fail to come up with answers that actually help your business, you read this book. Here you will find so many insights into things that you can do.

The opening chapter of the book gives us the author's own particular point of view. If you agree with him, fine, but, if you don't, avoid putting the book down. To do so would mean being unaware of how small firms can learn lessons from the brands and compete successfully against them.

Here are just half a dozen examples that I like. They are little things that really do make a difference, yet none are rocket science.

1. *'Sell with your ears and not with your mouth.'*
   How often have you been put off by someone who can't shut up and who isn't actually listening to what you – the customer – has to say?
2. *'If the telephone rings more than three times in your business, make it your business to answer it.'*
   The telephone is still the key tool for orders so it must be answered. Too many bosses think it demeaning to be answering the phone, but actually the customer loves it because they are speaking to the boss not a functionary from a brand. Equally importantly you learn what

is actually going on. Of course, afterwards you might enquire – ever so politely – of your staff why the phone was not answered.

3. *'If you have a corporate logo use it consistently, everywhere and forever.'*
The key to a good brand is the feeling that it generates of awareness, desirability and consistency. Yet it is far from impossible for a small firm also to generate similar qualities. How about, if you are in haulage, having white vehicles – always clean – with just your name and website address in small letters on the cab? After all, who can fail to be aware of Dyno-Rod's vans or the cleanliness of Eddie Stobart's lorries?

4. *'Put yourself in the mind of the customer and ask what they want.'*
Assume you have a small petrol station and are competing against Shell. What do you do? First, you put yourself in the mind of the customer who might be new to the area. This individual might want petrol, but might also want somewhere to eat or to stay. So why not advertise free maps, with local hotels and restaurants marked? You could attract more customers and, in the longer run, generate advertising revenue.

5. *'Use the media.'*
Of course every move by the 'brand names' is tracked and debated in the media. Just think back to the discussion about Pepsi turning blue! But too often small firms are either intimidated by the media or fail to see it as a selling opportunity. The crucial thing to remember is that journalists, whether local or national, have to fill their space. Frequently they are searching for stories, so why not provide them with something about your business? The media can be your friend.

6. *'Even cardboard boxes can be interesting.'*
What do you do to generate a brand image if you are a cardboard box manufacturer? Answer: put poems on the side of the box. The cost is minimal and the copyright on the older poems is over. But most important is that it generates an emotion and is memorable. It differentiates you from the crowd.

These six are, of course, mere illustrations and ones that particularly appeal to me. For many more, read on.

David Storey

Introduction

Branding does not exist outside of other, wider factors, whether they are social or environmental. In appealing to people in the way brands do, they are unconsciously tapping into widely held fears, beliefs, hopes and dreams. To understand and fully exploit the commercial opportunities for smaller business today, it is useful to look at the whole picture and comprehend how the role of business has changed and grown.

From 1945 to 1980, there was a highly destructive political battle fought in the UK between left and right. This brought our once proud economy to its knees. Neither side emerges with praise, but what particularly characterises the last twenty years is the melting of politics into a more or less background noise. And what has filled the vacuum of conflict and meaning that used to be provided by politics? Business and brands now compete for our attentions with as much loyalty and attention as politics used to muster.

Bigger brands have been having it their own way for the last twenty years. They can simply drive smaller businesses out of the picture by building low-cost, high-volume operations that smaller businesses cannot compete with. The only way to win that game is not to play. There is no such thing as a free lunch. By growing huge, many companies grow very boring. They lose the ability to delight. Only 15 per cent of the economy is food and shelter, while 85 per cent is fun. It is arguable that big businesses are getting worse and worse at delighting the senses and pleasing the mind. They are often ugly, not beautiful. There is a huge appetite for diverse, modern, friendly and alternative businesses. As people spend more time using the Internet, and less time watching TV, the power of advertising to dictate tastes, particularly among the wealthy, is diminishing.

It's important that we know how these impact before we try to apply them to smaller brands – and what better way to do this than to study the effects of the best-known and most influential brands in the world?

In Chapter 1, I examine the political and social context of business – in particular the emergent role of smaller businesses as a vital counterforce to the more unpleasant examples of big businesses. I analyse in some detail a few of those less pleasant aspects of big business and the effect they have on something that is very important to us all: the environment. You cannot divorce business – large or small – from the impact it has on our ecology, and, in most cases, it's big business that makes the big impact. And I make these points for a very good reason, other than a concern for our world: in a book called *It's Not About Size*, you would expect me to cite some of the ways in which small and medium businesses can score over their big brothers. By using the first part of Chapter 1 to put big business into an environmental context, I hope I can make the point much more cogently that it really *isn't* about size, and that small and medium enterprises can make a real impact for the good of all as well as themselves.

CHAPTER ONE

Businesses in the community

Chapter outline

In this chapter, we look at how smaller businesses used to dominate commerce, how things changed to suit big business, and how people now want to return to a more personal style of trade on a more human scale. We ask: is this a branding issue for small and medium enterprises (SMEs)?

Businesses in the community

Small businesses used to dominate commerce. Cottage industries used local materials and small teams of workers were involved in every stage of production. Then corporations emerged, built on the philosophy of mass production. Tasks were segmented and standardised in factory production lines and workers became alienated from the products they were involved in making and selling.

The mechanical efficiency with which large corporations deliver their products, and the consistency of what they offer their customers is unquestionable. But do customers really want everything to be the same? Has the world not become a little bland? However hard they might try, through centralised branding projects and rigorous staff training, our supermarkets just cannot achieve the charm, diversity, responsiveness and customer awareness that a well-run high street delicatessen can. But they do have a very potent weapon that they will use to continue their mission to rid our high streets of all character and diversity: price.

Small businesses cannot necessarily compete on price, but the tide of change is with them. Over time, smaller stores will again dominate our high streets, because big business is not only exceptionally dull, but is also often unsustainable and slow to react to consumer demand. Today, smaller companies must seize the opportunities that are arising from the failure of global corporations to meet the *human* requirements of creativity and community.

Many people think that the days of big business are numbered, and look at the opportunity that this presents for smaller business. How can the smaller business better meet the needs of today's consumers, and how can it win customers in the face of the massive advertising and marketing campaigns paid for from the deep pockets of big companies?

Big business

Big business is a disaster – one that is happening all over the world. Multinational corporations are like a bacteriological condition spreading out of control, with no known cure. Except perhaps for one dwindling counterforce: the smaller business.

If this seems like a shocking statement, let us examine the facts. From climate change to the long-hours culture, some multinational corporations farm us like livestock for the sole purpose of maximising profits. The financial community has actually elevated this careless barbarism into a financial philosophy. In many ways the achievements of the last hundred years have been spectacular. A billion cars have been produced, and a billion people have access to telephones.

But the runaway train is about to hit the buffers. The ice caps are melting, sea levels rising, storms are rendering parts of the world uninsurable – and all this against a background of unprecedented environmental destruction. Tens of thousands of species are made extinct, and our beautiful natural environment is irrevocably scarred in the name of 'economic development'.

The Norwegian philosopher Arne Naess, father of the deep-ecology movement, has stated the proposition succinctly: 'We must act now.'

Naess has a fascinating environmental and political philosophy which is encapsulated by the so called 'Apron diagram', because it has a drawstring in the middle.

This, very broadly, is how it goes:

1 You can think or believe anything
2 You must act within the limits of the ecosystem
3 You can, within these limits, do anything.

In 1995 at Schumacher College, Naess was interviewed and asked if he felt optimistic about the future. This grand old intellectual, who was made Professor of Philosophy at Stockholm University when he was only 25, smiled at the camera and said without blinking, 'I feel very optimistic about the twenty-second century.'

Sustainable development

Sustainable development is the formal name for, in the words of Chris Patten in his 2000 BBC Reith lecture on the subject of Governance, living here on earth, 'as though we were intending to stay for good, not just visit for the week-end'. This may come as a shock, but it is true to say that many multinational companies simply do not have the intelligence required to make the world sustainable. Their relationships with customers are totally inhuman. There is no Mr Texaco, or Ms Burger King. And, even where there is a Sainsbury or Dell behind the name, you tend not to bump into them when you go shopping.

Because big companies have no meaningful relationship with customers, a culture has grown up globally whereby they do not care about you, and you do not care about them. Don't get me wrong. The people working for multinationals aren't consciously trying to destroy the world: it's just that they're caught in a destructive trap which only small businesses can stop. Remember that, ultimately, it is customers who have power.

Lowering prices or increasing volumes for ever cannot successfully maximise our happiness as if we were machines with infinite capacity to consume. What makes us happy is style, beauty, a positive attitude and pleasing experiences. Neither the accountant nor the engineer can deliver these alone. Truly successful, sustainable businesses need to recognise the contribution of designers, architects, stylists and other specialists in human factors who can better honour the inherent potential for growth and dignity in the life of mankind.

Today we see some extremes of pleasing customers. For so-called 'first-class' passengers – harking back to the Victorian era – on some airlines, cabin crew can be fired or fêted on the slightest frown or smile from a traveller. (Just take a look at the court cases raging between airlines and members of their crews around the subject of constructive dismissal.) But, if that traveller gets even better service with a lower price from another airline, they will move.

This whole system is brutally efficient and incredibly cynical. It is about maximising returns for shareholders, and we customers and our real hopes and dreams really do not matter. The vapidity of multinational business has become entirely socially acceptable. Learned journals such as the *Harvard Business Review* use scientific methodology to explain how the most financially successful companies succeed in extracting the most money from people. But that is the end of the debate – full stop. I have sat in many meetings where some clown or other has delighted in reminding us that it is all about making money. And certainly it used to be. But not any more.

The death of the corporations

Very large companies have simply lost their licence to operate, their credibility and the public trust. This will be the century of the smaller business, however unlikely that may seem today. In her book *Beyond Globalization: Shaping a Sustainable Global Economy*, November 1999, the brilliant futurist Hazel Henderson has described international finance today as, 'the politics of the last hurrah'. What she is alluding to is the blaringly loud and triumphalist tone of so many communications from the capitalist elite. Advertising from merchant banks provides a good example of this. Their messages of ceaseless multinational growth are so obviously alien and antithetical to the requirements of a sustainable world, where energy and natural resources are conserved and not squandered, that they sound like screeching adolescent boys.

Our world and the ecosystems that make it divine are incredibly intricate. Multinational companies have conspired, if unwittingly, to exploit our planet to the point where it is close to death. Be in no doubt about this. The Intergovernmental Panel on Climate Change (IPCC) see devastating consequences in the near future. Andrew Dlugoleksi, an executive director of CGNU (formerly Commercial

General Norwich Union), the UK's largest insurance company, commented in November 2000 that the world economy would become bankrupted by climate change by 2056.

It is interesting to note that the first warning of the dangers of DDT (dichlorodiphenyltrichloroethane) build-up resulted from the brilliant invention of the gas spectrometer by James Lovelock. It was the American marine biologist Rachel Carson who sounded the first public warning of an impending catastrophe with her chilling book *Silent Spring* in 1962. Lovelock went on to work for NASA to consider life on Mars. Looking at this dead planet, he came to consider our own world. Having established that the sun had become 30 per cent hotter over the last 3,500 million years, he was amazed to discover that the earth had stayed at approximately the same temperature during this period. This was evidence that Earth has a self-regulating climate system. His next-door neighbour, the novelist William Golding, suggested he name this process Gaia.

As long ago as 1999, scientists from the UK Government's Hadley Centre researching Climate Change, predicted global warming will cause 'substantial dieback of tropical forests and tropical grasslands ... by the 2080s, especially in parts of northern South America and central southern Africa'. This will turn hundreds of millions of acres of South American rainforest into desert by the end of this century. And, if we could somehow miraculously stop climate change, the sea would still be devoid of fish, the rainforests would still be gone, and so on and so on.

The sustainability crisis

Dr Jeremy Leggett is Charterhouse Fellow in Solar Energy at Oxford University's Environmental Change Unit. He comments on the issue in his book *The Carbon War* (2000) as follows:

> The IPCC has announced that it will make sudden and chaotic climate change a central feature of its third report, due out in 2001. IPCC scientists seem unwilling to wait until 2001, and it is little wonder. Just before the last Christmas of the century, the chief meteorologists of the US and UK took the unusual step of writing to national newspapers to say that recent work of their agencies 'confirms that our climate is changing rapidly'. The situation, they warned, is critical.

It is becoming so obvious now. The ice shelves on the Antarctic Peninsular are in full retreat, having lost 3,000 square kilometres (1,160 square miles) of ice in 1998 alone. An early draft of the third IPCC report concludes that a 3°C warming over Greenland would make melting the ice cap irreversible, meaning a 7-metre (23-foot) rise in global sea level over the next millennium. The worst storm in two centuries hit France on Boxing Day 1999. More than 100 million trees fell.

In newspapers the story is the same. For example, in 1998, Environment Minister Michael Meacher said: 'Millions of people will have life made miserable by climate change, with increased risk of hunger, water shortages and extreme events like flooding. Combating climate change is the greatest challenge of human history.'

Ritt Bjerregaard, Member of the European Commission responsible for the Environment has said, 'We need to develop new technologies. And we must ensure changes in the public's attitude, which is so crucial. We must reduce our carbon dependency. There is no way to avoid that.'

In 1999 the Red Cross warned on climate change, saying that the developed countries' polluting lifestyles represented a massive debt owed to the poor. Commenting on their report, the July 1999 edition of Insurance Day said, 'Fires, droughts and floods from last year's El Niño claimed 21,000 lives while the deforestation in China's Yangtze basin contributed to the flooding which affected the lives of 180m people.

'In Russia, the extreme winter weather turned into a disaster when it struck a society where 44m people are living in poverty, 1m children are homeless, and tuberculosis rates are skyrocketing.

'This insidious combination is throwing millions more into the path of potential disaster. Already, 96% of all deaths from natural disasters occur in developing countries . . . With tides forecast to creep up 44 cm by 2080, hundreds of millions of the planet's inhabitants living in coastal megacities and small island states are threatened.'

On 17 June 2000 the *Financial Times* stated: 'The Royal Commission on Environmental Pollution yesterday called for a "complete transformation in the UK's use of energy" in what it called one of the most important reports in its 30-year history.

'It urged the UK to plan for a 60 per cent cut in the carbon dioxide produced by burning fossil fuels over the next 50 years, as an essential part of the global response to climate change.

'"We cannot expect other nations to do their part in countering this threat – least of all if they are much less wealthy – unless we demonstrate we are really serious about it," said Sir Tom Blundell, commission chairman.'

In 1999, Thomas Goreau, president of the Global Coral Reef Alliance, and foremost world expert on corals, was quoted in the *Independent* on 13 November 1998, where he described global warming as 'an unprecedented natural disaster'. He said 'Coral reefs are the most sensitive ecosystem of all to temperature increase. They are like the canary in the mine. They are the first ecosystem that will go and right now they can't take any – any – more warming.'

We've lost the plot

How is this being allowed to happen? Big business is out of control, that's how. It's ironic that, just as the environment has come to play a larger part in the global consciousness and has become increasingly absorbed into many more aspects of decision making, so we seem to have lost the plot. We cannot see the wood for the trees. Yes, environmental concerns are factored into decision making, but there's compromise at almost every turn, and so it seems we've developed a mechanism whereby all can stand up and display their green credentials, while the reality is that our natural resource base is still suffering death by a thousand cuts, being eroded by millions of micro-decisions and micro-compromises the world over.

Small wonder, then, that sparrow numbers fall. To name but one species.

To attend to this giant problem, we need hundreds of thousands of heads on the case. Only smaller businesses can find the millions of practical and sustainable requirements for the twenty-first-century lifestyle.

As the Prime Minister, Tony Blair, said in a speech to the CBI on 24 October 2000, 'We have to face a stark fact: neither we here in Britain, nor our partners abroad, have succeeded in reversing the overall destructive trend.

'The truth is, these problems are more urgent and more pressing than they have ever been and the solutions at the moment do not measure up to the scale of the problem. It is a very big issue for us.'

We have to pursue new avenues for solutions that overcome the contemporary power vacuum and mobilise people, businesses and politicians in substantial ways. As *The Economist* said in a 2000 commentary on climate change, the solutions are to be found in harnessing the engine of economic growth and the ingenuity of entrepreneurs.

And what are the messages of the future? *No* to burning carbon, *yes* to solar energy, *no* to wholesale transport of goods, *yes* to wholesale transport of information. Let's be absolutely clear: this is about a strategy for economic growth and it is the only strategy that has any chance of delivering what we all want for ourselves and others. If everyone in the world lived the same lifestyle as those of us in the US and the UK currently do, we would need three planets to sustain us.

So think of the potential for new, emerging businesses to grow by getting behind climate-friendly solutions. The trick is to achieve critical mass in the way the railway pioneers did in the nineteenth century with the creation of connecting networks, or the information revolution of the last century and this. In both cases it is about entrepreneurs' commitment to creating a critical mass of capacity and connections. The formal definition of this effect is expressed in Metcalf's Law. The inventor of the Ethernet computer communication protocol formulated the principle that 'The utility of networks increases by the square of the number of users.' This same principle applies exactly to low carbon economic developments such as videoconferencing, fuel cell or solar power production. Scale achieves economies and creates breakthrough to the mass market. This is from long-term, not short-term, investment and gives big rewards for the wait. The same thing applies to such things as car-sharing networks, small-scale electricity production and storage, and new transit networks.

Tessa Tennant is the genius behind socially responsible investment in the UK. She pioneered the first-ever sustainable investment fund in the UK at Jupiter Asset Management from 1988–1994, and was Director of Sustainable Responsible Investment (SRI) at NPI Hendersons between 1994 and 2000.

She is also a Member of the UK Government's Advisory Committee on Business and the Environment, an Adviser to the United Nations Environment Programme Finance Initiative, a Trustee of Friends of the Earth, UK, a WWF ambassador, and a co-founder of the UK Social Investment Forum (Chair from 1993–1997).

She has developed some powerful proposals, delivered to Tony Blair in her speech at 10 Downing Street on 4 December 2000, see www.number-10.gov.uk/default.asp?PageID=2935. She believes that to help facilitate the transition smaller businesses require governments worldwide to sign up for the following commitments to be achieved by the 2012 Earth Summit:

> ■ ensuring that there is a sustainable investment option for every saver on the planet
>
> ■ ensuring access to finance on reasonable terms for every individual on the planet, thereby helping directly to remove one of the greatest indictments of our times, namely the numbers of people in our own country and elsewhere still in poverty

Smaller businesses need to grow, fast, and help repair the miserable and conflicting messages given by so many big companies' communications to so many people. As much as we are exhorted by the government to save energy, the overall message is that life continues as normal, reinforced by other messages, primarily through corporate advertising that encourages us to buy the new breed of gas guzzler, fly to exotic places for every holiday and earn more and more air miles. It's worth remembering that big corporations worldwide spend $300 billion each year on advertising alone. This is a conflict in communications. Small wonder there's a muddle in the public mind, which itself results in greater resistance to change.

The response of multinationals is fascinating. The oil company whose formal name is BP Amoco have declared that their initials no longer stand for 'British Petroleum', but rather 'Beyond Petroleum'. They are indicating the end of their core product. It may shock some readers to realise that BP have thought this far ahead. But they know how bad the situation is. More than 99 per cent of the atmosphere is oxygen and nitrogen but, as Sir John Houghton, FRS, observes in his 1997 book *Global Warming*, these gases 'neither absorb nor emit thermal radiation' – it is carbon dioxide present in the atmosphere that threatens our species. Therefore, since burning petroleum creates almost 100 per cent carbon dioxide, even BP realise that we must all move 'beyond petroleum'.

Another great contributor to climate change, Shell, is spending tens of millions of dollars in advertising stating that it is committed to sustainable development. That is an odd message for one of the three largest oil companies, chief agents of unsustainable development.

I have spent my whole career working as a communications consultant for multinationals, including Shell. The people who run these companies are OK, they're nice folk. But their organisations are so completely unable to repair the damage they do. It would be laughable were it not so tragic.

Diversity

Diversity is a small word that underpins a very, very big idea. It is very easy for large-scale, scientifically designed systems to reduce diversity. This process tends to increase the aggregate total output of one thing, typically the thing that makes money. But that is not always a happy process. The out-of-town superstore has everything we want (or so we are told), but the cost is a reduction in high street shopping, socialising and community. A restaurant chain may find a very low-cost formula for delivering food fast, but goodbye to the *local* restaurant – and healthy food. I eat at McDonald's sometimes; it is cheap and easy. But if every restaurant were a McDonald's we might not be so happy.

Diversity is key, and smaller food outlets can borrow some of the tricks from McDonald's without coming to symbolise the homogenisation of culture that so many people dislike. Fish-and-chip shops are just as inexpensive, and fast.

So let us sum up some of the things that are wrong with the way business is today:

Too much commuting

According to Personal Travel Factsheet 3, June 1999, from the Department of the Environment, Transport and the Regions, the average distance between home and work increased by a third from 6.1 miles (9.81 kilometres) in 1985/86 to 8.1 miles (13.03 kilometres) in 1995/97. The average journey to work in 1998 took 25 minutes, compared with 23 minutes in 1993.

Too little variety and spontaneity

A relaxed atmosphere where good-natured jokes and laughter are heard often reflects a positive environment. The atmosphere is perceived as easy-going and light-hearted. The dull offices of too many large corporations lack good-natured joking and light-hearted banter. People become bored and uninspired by their work and so do not innovate.

Too many manufactured goods

In its 'Living Planet Report 2000', an assessment of the health of the world's environment, the Worldwide Fund for Nature (WWF) says humans are pushing the planet beyond its capacity. The amount of natural resources needed to provide such things as food, energy and manufactured goods, even at today's levels of economic activity, is 30 per cent above what the earth can provide without suffering serious damage.

Too little co-operation and sharing

Co-operation and sharing of information within organisations is essential if people are to achieve results at work. Yet cultures of secrecy all too often predominate, creating unnecessary stress and disillusionment and inhibiting any chances of providing customer satisfaction.

Each of the above problems contains a host of business opportunities. At root these problems present us with one basic question. Do we want to follow and idolise global companies, or grow our own? To follow is to be always behind, but building your own business is about taking control and deciding where you are going. And that will always put you ahead.

Business in the community

There is an organisation in the UK called Business in the Community. It concerns itself with encouraging and advising large companies on how best to spend a percentage of profits on 'community support'. Sometimes this activity is referred to as 'putting something back'.

The converse of that phrase succinctly reveals the practical consequence of today's large-scale business activity. Essentially, they are *taking something out* of the communities in which they operate. But, at another level, they are doing worse than that. A business that reaches into a community from outside, as an alien entity, does more than just extract cash: it disempowers people.

Over the last forty years we have given up on the local electrical shop, butcher, baker, fruit-and-veg seller and smaller restaurants. Why? Because the larger concerns were simply better in so many ways. Here is a short list of where they excelled:

- More access to capital for investment.
- Advantages of scale in advertising development, as this could be shared among more branches (bulk purchase of advertising space and airtime also achieved discounts).
- High-quality design. Expensive to buy once, but reusable across a large number of outlets and even many countries. I have personally witnessed the incredible care and energy Shell took before rebranding more than 20,000 petrol stations.
- Greater central administration permitting more research into where and what to buy, volume discounts and scale efficiencies in logistics across all activities, distribution, finance and so on.
- Quality information acquisition and processing. Across many branch offices, different approaches could be tried experimentally and data gathered on what sells best. A large company is like a huge research programme designed to get the most money out of consumers. This is how 'best practice' develops across a big company. Successful local initiatives are rolled out across the whole estate.

Co-operate, collaborate

Smaller businesses will not be able to enjoy such advantages until they increase co-operation and collaboration. The purpose of a big company is in fact similar to that of a local community. But big businesses operate nationally or internationally. Internally they foster co-operation and thrive on interdependence, all for the company. They are centrally planned, vast organisms.

Why have local businesses so far not been able to oppose the onslaught of bigger companies?

- Smaller businesses had no scale with which to respond.
- They looked dated and therefore somehow ugly, or at least uninteresting.
- Self-service appealed to busy people who preferred not to get caught up in the chatter associated with small shops and friendly shopkeepers.

Before going on to examine the individual perceived shortcomings of yesterday's smaller businesses, let's look at this last point in detail. In the UK, we have always said we had, or have talked about, a class system. This, or the perception of it, has certainly contributed to the catastrophic decline of UK industry since World War Two. In essence, our industry declined because bosses and workers harboured mutual suspicion and were less inclined to co-operate. Self service in part developed to allow British people to avoid their numerous antagonisms of 'status' and 'class'. Because we could not cope with each other, we just avoided each other instead.

If this seems like an extreme statement, look at the decades of industrial action, culminating in the so-called 'winter of discontent' that ushered in Margaret Thatcher and her rather right-wing government in 1979. Nationalised business had reached a point whereby collectively organised workers and management simply could not co-operate. Horrible factories and buildings were part of the problem. The business guru Charles Handy said in *Management Today*, November 1997, 'Atmosphere makes more difference than any number of logos. Boring places breed boring thoughts and boring people, of that I am sure, and then the one feeds on the other to produce yet more boring spaces.

'Quality and style however, encourage quality and style in their inhabitants.

'It is hard to produce shoddy work in a beautiful place, where even the functional necessities are elegant. Buildings and offices often wear their hearts on their sleeves. You can tell what life is like within them just by taking a look at them.'

How different is the German model, where a representative of the 'workers' will sit on the board of directors of most large companies. The genius of postwar Germany – and the idiocy of postwar Britain – relate to the success or failure of companies to create a sense of common purpose that permeates the entire organisation.

In the UK we can perceive class even in people's accents, which can colour our first impressions. So we find ourselves in a country that observes polite customs such as saying please and thank you, while we're often at one another's throat. This comedy of manners and unjustified resentment undermines our ability to communicate normally.

The short story is that Britain has emerged from a period of protracted internal friction, real or imagined, into a society that craves, at least in its business undertakings, anonymity. We have learned to deal with our clumsy manners and awkwardness by developing a culture of avoiding contact altogether. So when companies such as Sainsbury's and Shell started pioneering self-service, consumers leapt at the chance to escape the awkwardness of contact.

How, then, can a smaller business deal with this problem? Here are a few ideas for dealing with icy customers:

- Make more of what you do self-service, and put the magic words 'self-service' on your signs.

- Make sure you and your colleagues wear name badges with your first name clearly visible. This shows you are, at least in principle, prepared to be friendly and approachable. The former chief executive of Asda Group, Archie Norman, took over running the company when it was lost and in the doldrums. Early in his tenure he started wearing a big green badge saying 'Archie'. It was hard for other staff members not to follow suit!

- A simple technique for saving customers from feeling that they are about to be jumped on by a member of staff is to have a sign saying, 'Please feel free to browse'.

- *Never, ever* let anyone stand in the doorway of your premises. Nobody will come in so long as someone lurks there.

- If a customer walks up to a colleague while you're chatting to her, say, 'I'll tell you later', and discreetly move away. Don't keep the customer waiting. Customers pay your wages, so look upon them as the bosses' bosses.

Overall, remember that a customer is a stranger. You know nothing whatsoever about them. Try not to judge the way they look or dress. Maybe a staggeringly drunk person is unwelcome, and should be shown the door quickly. But someone in builders' clothes could easily afford something expensive. If you are serving wine in a restaurant, don't automatically offer it to the man to taste. That will insult many women and men. Any racist, homophobic or sexist attitude to any customer on any occasion can destroy your reputation for ever. Don't do it.

Just treat each new customer as someone who might slowly, in their own time, spend a lot of money with you. It is a good idea to match them conversationally. If they are a bit shy, you should not seem to be overbearing. Some people say, and I agree, that you sell with your ears, and not your mouth. So, if you have time and the customer wants to tell you what they want, take time to listen. Above all, just act naturally.

So let's look at some other reasons why smaller local businesses get slaughtered by bigger companies.

Need to innovate

We are a clever species, we humans. Consumers expect improvement. That does not mean buying new fixtures and fittings every three months, but for a shop it may mean spending time and energy looking at your window display. Perhaps every month. Take a little time out. Look at the windows of your competitors and top city-centre shops. Think about designs for improvement. The trick is to do a lot with a little money. Let your competitors try to seduce customers with the marketing equivalent of a diamond gold ring. But see how seductive *you* can be with one red rose.

A theme we will return to again is that in so much design, advertising and communications, less is more. It's not about size, but what you do with it.

Localisation is your most powerful friend. So, if your company has operated at the same location for twenty years, you can say that. Try making a sign that says, 'Drake's Bar and Grill, in our street for twenty years. Try the best in town.'

This approach will not always help. For a hairdresser it probably would not work. Why? Because hairdressers need to appear new to seem fashionable. But for a restaurant it could work well to stress pedigree.

I am not an advertising copywriter but do know how it is done. A good advertising copywriter will write out perhaps two hundred slogans while trying to find the right one. They often work in teams, and try to build on each other's work. Or rip it apart, in the spirit of stress testing. (Incidentally, this is what teams of people are good at. Monty Python, the highly successful comedy group, were famous for long meetings at which they tried their best to rubbish each other's ideas.)

The point about the Drake's bar sign is that it say's 'Bar and Grill'. People know that means you sell alcohol and meat, a popular combination. Does it matter if Drake's got a grill only last month? No. Does it matter if you don't have a bar? Well, if your licence allows you to sell casual drinks, then the answer is again no. When the sign says 'in our street for twenty years' it's proving to customers that it must be getting something right. And when it says, 'Try the best in our town' it is perhaps reassuring the visitor that the place is not an exclusive and private venue that does not welcome visitors.

But the key point behind this sign is that a new chain cannot make this claim. So find your strength, your uniqueness, and emphasise it. One of the reasons local businesses have failed is that they do not grasp their unique advantages, and leverage them.

Product quality

Another reason for the decline in local business is that multiple or other giant business can simply offer better products, more cheaply. This is the crux of the whole war. To combat this trend you will have to do some pioneering. Let us consider an example of businesses that have really suffered at the hands of larger concerns, and a possible response.

Food shops and sandwich bars

Local food shops have simply not got the range, the overseas contacts and the market power to provide strawberries from California and runner beans from Africa. They do not have parking facilities and the convenience of multiple purchasing opportunities. So what can be done? Well, there are many strategies that can be adopted.

Go green

By far the bigger margins in food today are taken by purveyors of 'organics'. Why is this? Consumers do not trust food manufacturers, they are more conscious of health and, in addition to the occasional food-poisoning scare, there tends to be a suspicion of high levels of pesticides and herbicides and genetically modified organisms.

But consumer tastes don't change by accident. People are made to change. The big supermarkets simply started selling strawberries from California and runner beans from Africa. And we were seduced into buying them because they looked great and were cheap. But how clever is it to use aeroplanes to exploit low wages in other countries? To many, that smacks of reckless energy consumption – and it can be exploited very effectively. It was the economist John Maynard Keynes (1883–1946) who said, 'It is better to export recipes than cakes.' That basic truth plays straight into the hands of smaller business.

So the question is: Can you seduce people into buying from you because your food is sourced locally? This may seem an impossible job, or maybe it is rather easy. Let us look at some of the ugly aspects of multiple or global companies:

- Smaller businesses use fewer natural resources.
- Smaller businesses use less energy.
- Smaller businesses make for variety on the high street, rather than the homogeneity that's often evident throughout a store chain's operations.
- Smaller businesses tend not to strive for employing as few people as they can get away with.

Any of the points on this list could and should make powerful ammunition for hard-hitting marketing campaigns. To illustrate this point, let's just take one. The use of energy.

Since the nationwide flooding in the UK in October/November 2000, ministers have been telling the public about the horrors of climate change. Gerhard Berz, head of the geo-science research group at Munich Re, one of the world's largest insurance companies, commentated on 29 December 2000, 'Global warming has to be slowed down. Otherwise the risk situation for insurers in many of the world's regions will intensify.'

It would soon become clear from this that a major change is required by society. One key aspect relates to movement of goods, especially by air. It is in my view unacceptable for anyone to transport goods by air, especially fast-moving consumer goods such as food. The volumes involved in transportation of perishable items, like food and fresh flowers provide a massive and growing component of air freight, a most energy-intensive activity.

Mark Mansley, author of *Socially Responsible Investment: a Guide for Pension Funds and Institutional Investors* (2000) and an expert in ethical investment, has suggested that close analysis of the distance our food travels to our tables may result in the shocking truth that it is more environmentally friendly to drive than walk: the more energy we expend in walking, the more food we are likely to consume – food that will probably have been transported by air.

Make customers care

So how can you persuade consumers really to care about climate change and food miles? The secret is to tackle the problem on two fronts. First, find food producers as near as possible to where you are. Ten miles is best. Within fifty miles is good. Perhaps from within your county. Maybe it could even be that you kick off the process whereby UK counties begin to label goods they supply as 'Yorkshire fresh' or 'Sussex fresh' so people get to know exactly where things come from.

Second, think about advertising. And this need not cost too much. Especially if you are clever. Let me cite a couple of examples. An Australian entrepreneur called Dick Smith is a recognised expert in low-budget publicity. He tells great stories of how to grab the public's attention. One of the first things he did was to make a small plastic 'iceberg' out of odds and ends, paint it white, then use a small boat with his company's name on the side to drag it into Sydney Harbour. Next, he got all his staff to phone the local radio stations and say, 'Someone's towing an iceberg into Sydney Harbour.' Dick Smith created an amusing story that gave people a change from their day-to-day humdrum news stories.

In another low-budget act of genius, Smith put an advert in the newspaper, for a few hundred dollars, saying, 'Man wanted to go into mountains for three months eating only Dick Smith peanut butter.' Not only did this odd request gather more than thirty applicants, it also drew a huge amount of publicity as journalists tried to work out what it was all about.

Now you may think it is easier to make odd jokes about icebergs and peanut butter than it is to get people interested in organic food (and, through that, maybe in climate change). But maybe that's not true. If you source food locally and organically, a lot of information will come your way. So what can you do with it?

Catch 'em young

One thing you can do is communicate with schools. It is a tried and tested tactic of many very large hamburger purveyors to present themselves primarily as children's entertainers. They work on the assumption that, if you get the children to visit, the adults will follow. And a generation that visits your restaurant or shop as children will continue to do so as adults. Could you come up with content or educational information that is as compelling as a clown or some other cartoon entertainment?

Bright red, yellow and green plastic interiors, combined with food that is full of sugar and fat, makes a formula that is very hard to beat. Children love fast food. If you are close to your community, and suppliers of food, think what organising a trip to a farm might do to compete with that? Local schools Parent Teacher Associations should be able to find volunteers to assist in managing a visit including many delights:

- Kids love to make food. It is like mud pies you can eat!
- They love to pick strawberries and raspberries.
- They love to dig up carrots and radishes.
- It is fun to make sugary scones, toffee apples and other treats.
- Fast-food companies give away small collectable gifts. These tend to be inexpensive, so try to develop your own.
- Getting some distribution together so a locally – or at least regionally – produced range of snacks make their way into school tuck boxes.

The success of fast-food chains in influencing children is considerable. We can even admire their success. But there is, as they say, more than one way to skin a cat. The experiences children take from consuming fast food are immediate and repetitive. However, children are also very flexible and willing to learn, change and adapt. In fact children are genetically programmed to want to learn – although it may not seem like that sometimes!

By offering diversity and variety, by helping introduce children to memorable experiences that are unpredictable, you can help them to develop a wider vocabulary of more sophisticated tastes. And that should mean more business for local organic-food providers.

To summarise approaches to children:

- Think of what information you can gather about local, or reasonably close, food suppliers.
- What data can you gather about organics?
- How can you network with schools, perhaps through parent–teacher associations or school governors?
- Is there a way to get kids to visit farms?

> How can you co-operate with local food producers to get kids interested in your products through field trips or other exercises?

It has been suggested that it would be pretty much impossible to get people to visit farms but I disagree. Notwithstanding the 2001 Foot and Mouth epidemic, when it is safe to visit farms, nothing stands between you and organising a trip. If you think it impossible remember the following:

- UK households spend an average four hours per day watching television.
- Car ownership is at an all time high.
- Community leaders of all kinds protest that youth are increasingly inward and disconnected from the external world, playing TV games and losing social skills.
- The UK is the fourth most wealthy country in the entire world. If we cannot organise some trips to the country for children to learn about life, what they eat and where it comes from, God help us.

Remember that, although this activity may take time to turn into sales, you should see it as an investment and it should be fun. You will win new customers for life. And, best of all, none of the big companies will be able to copy you. That is simply not what they are set up to do.

What about adults?
What techniques can be used to stimulate adults' interest in, and appetite for, local food and organic produce?

People have a gut sense of right and wrong. Not everybody but most. When I ask people in larger stores where a food comes from, if it is foreign, they usually say something like, 'It's from overseas – isn't that awful?' So if we accept that, at a fundamental level, people know that importing 'fresh food' is wrong, what can you do? A few powerful slogans might be:

NO FLOWN FOOD

ACT GLOBAL, SPEND LOCAL

CLIMATE-SAFE FOOD

Familiarity breeds boredom

Believe it or not, people are terribly bored by the suffocating similarity of modern big businesses. There has even been a move by some UK local authorities to partner with small businesses to reduce the blandness of city centres. A friend of mine called Matthew Dennis is an art lecturer, award-winning designer and satirist. He refers to such towns as 'CarParkChester', and that is the ugly reality of most British towns and cities. Expensively developed shopping areas have been introduced that are usually pedestrianised. They are typically vehicles for a not unfamiliar bevy of retailers. Woolworth's, Safeway, Boots, WH Smith, Marks & Spencer, the odd bank. Have we forgotten anybody?

These businesses are all built on the same wholly unsustainable principles. Their products are sourced from thousands of geographically dispersed suppliers. They pay zero attention to many crucial issues such as:

- the energy involved in manufacture
- volume of unnecessary packaging
- impact on local or regional economy

Addressing these themes can give you a fertile territory in which to operate. The first step is to work out all the different messages you could be communicating, then try to work them into one key theme.

- Locally produced food.
- Good for you.
- Good for the local economy.
- Good for the environment (fewer food miles).

Now think of fifty or more possible succinct brands, themes, slogans or messages. Assuming your store is located in a town called Aldeburgh in Suffolk, or you have a few stores in Suffolk, try to combine the ideas and location. Suffolk Organics, Suffolk Foods, Fresh and Local, Aldeburgh Organics, Suffolk Farms, Aldeburgh Farms, Frankenstein Free, Healthy Local, Healthy Suffolk, Pride of Suffolk, Suffolk Economic Foods, Aldeburgh Economy Foods, Local Action Foods, Aldeburgh Health, Local Wealth . . .

And so on. Try to come up with a hundred names or more. Then choose the few best ones, and try them out on friendly customers. From the short list above I like the following ones for the following reasons:

Healthy Suffolk

This name or brand has a useful double meaning. It says the shop is 'healthy', a word we tend to apply mainly to food, but it also says Suffolk. And the literal meaning is that the county of Suffolk is healthy. If you choose this brand, you could register the name, develop a logo for 'Healthy Suffolk', and offer it to other stores in Suffolk who follow your principles. You do not necessarily have to charge money for the brand. You will control it, and build a presence without having to build a big central infrastructure.

This would be similar to a big company expanding by franchising, but more co-operative. You would have the right to remove the use of the brand from people so you can control quality, but you would not be stifling local innovation by making them run businesses your way. If well managed, 'Healthy Suffolk' might get a reputation for high quality, but also extreme diversity across many shops. A clear case of all for one and one for all. If you find monitoring the quality of participating shops too difficult, you could always share that duty with the shopkeepers you trust. You can learn more about this exciting area of franchising from books such as *Franchising for Dummies* (2000) by Dave Thomas and Michael Seid.

The above ideas might all just seem like extra work, but try to think of them instead as a social opportunity. Maybe such policies would provide a great reason to meet up regularly with your new colleagues for dinner or a chat over a drink. Remember that two great businesses, Lloyd's Bank and Lloyd's of London, grew out of Lloyd's coffee shop in the city.

Suffolk Economic Foods

This is another name from our list that may have some merit. Although rather too long at three words, the phrase has a ring to it. Perhaps it would draw shoppers into your store to find out more. It suggests low prices but perhaps also other ideas.

Planning a communications programme

Having spent what seems like far too long on choosing a name from hundreds of possibilities, then testing it out on people, and checking nobody else is using it, it is time to pull your communications programme together:

- Review all your strengths, weaknesses, opportunities and threats. Just write down four lists.
- List all the unique advantages you have over big multiple companies.
- Consider your competitors.
- Look at the areas in which you operate.
- Make a searching review of your customers – what are their key characteristics? For instance, who are your most profitable customers, and where do your customers come from?
- Ask yourself who are the potential customers you are most eager to acquire.

Having conducted this exercise, test the name again against your communications plan. Does it fit? Is it a good idea to repeat the exercise? If so, write down one hundred more names. How, if at all, has your thinking changed?

We have now had a quick, roller-coaster review of how your company fits into the community, and how it is perceived. Now we will look in detail at the components of branding.

CHAPTER TWO

Understanding a brand

Chapter outline

In this chapter we will examine what branding can really do, and what it can't. A large element of branding is about consistency. So we need to ask why continuity of service is key, and how achieving this goal may involve a commitment to more effective job training for all staff.

How to give your business a personality

It has been said that, if a person has style, it is something they never think about. The implication here is that style is an intrinsic characteristic that cannot be acquired. Like physical beauty, style is a positive attribute that we look for in those we encounter. We like it when we see it.

Thomas Frank, author of *The Conquest of Cool* (University of Chicago Press, Chicago, 1997), has suggested that the idea of 'cool', which emerged in the 1960s, has been appropriated as the official style of our business civilisation. Originally, the cool symbolised by James Dean and Jimmi Hendrix was a revolt against the existing order and it was revered as the next, better iteration of our society's development. However, at this political juncture, famously described as 'the end of history' by Francis Fukuyama (*The End of History and the Last Man*, Hamilton, London, 1992), there is nothing new ahead except bigger companies with more power. They will perhaps provide for both the mainstream and its alternative. In Frank's words,

The over-arching facts of economic life are that the society we live in is exploitative and joyless, but [corporate cool] also offers us this ready-made opposition that you can buy off the rack. Globalisation and the triumph of markets world-wide is resulting in this sort of conflict between the 'hip' and the 'square'. This conflict is replacing older social conflicts like those between the workers and owners. That is the genius of this ideology, the sort of bogus conflict between hip and square is all over the world now, it is the international language of advertising.

Smaller businesses can expose the cynicism intrinsic in this kind of marketing. They can show how consumers are being manipulated, and offer something authentic and different. Really different. Something authentically local. In achieving this, they can take from bigger businesses their greatest power: the ability to control our minds.

We need to think a bit bigger, and think a bit more. If we cannot develop innovative local retailing, we probably deserve the Boots, Woolworth's, Burger King and whatever else they dump on us. A true, vibrant, local business will come from a pedigree of care and innovation. So lesson one is to watch less TV. Lesson two is to think more, travel more and look at other people's shops. Buy magazines about design. Think about their contents. Above all, believe in your own ability to make a great business, and just do it.

The fact is that even the greatest corporations cannot make money from creating and selling art, or encouraging activities with cult followings such as snowboarding or skateboarding. Even with their billions of dollars they cannot lead youth culture or inspire love or affection, which means that a great proportion of human ingenuity and invention will perpetually lie outside their capabilities.

You can acquire the really interesting bit. You can use business to turn human ingenuity into a meaningful future. A smaller business does not have to suit everyone, appear bland, and just 'fit-in', using vast electric signs. There may be more sophisticated and successful ways to fit in with your local area, and to be 'cool'.

What's so hot about 'cool'?

So what is 'cool'? The American media analyst Sara Vowell describes cool as comprising two essential components: a sense of justice and a sense of humour. When you know what justice is, it means you have a heart; and, when you have a sense of humour, it means you have a brain.

Vowell believes that, in today's world, caring is the brave thing and it communicates authenticity. Genuineness is important because you can tell when an organisation is lying to you. Trust is the key element in generating social capital.

Although it can be easy to tire of what the great media analyst Marshall McLuhan called the 'ceaseless barrage of advertising messages which daily assault us', the UK is in many ways lucky. We have a visual culture that is capable of being spectacularly innovative and stimulating. UK dominance in pop culture, music and fashion testifies to this. The Australian-born writer and feminist Germaine Greer has described marketing as the great cultural phenomenon of our times. How can you use the power of business to communicate in a way that raises the grim tone of commerce? We cannot let giant corporations stitch up what we are really about. In the words of David Korten in his chilling book *When Corporations Rule the World* (Earthscan, London, 1995),

> When control of our cultural symbols passes to corporations, we are essentially yielding to them the power to define who we are. Instead of being Americans, Norwegians, Egyptians, Filipinos, or Mexicans, we become simply members of the 'Pepsi generation', detached from place and any meaning other than those a corporation finds it profitable to confer on us.

The outrageous attempt to shepherd us like sheep has ground down the validity of large corporations. They are ready to be dealt a blow. It is time for smaller businesses to develop bigger brands, and capitalise on the cynicism and despair of local people who are, after all, everybody.

Mind games

It is frightening the way corporations control our minds. In a similar process, just as some languages in equatorial regions have no word for snow because the population has never encountered it, so it is with aesthetics. The dominant organisations employing the power of artists to promote their interests control in many ways the very vocabulary of thought. The global dream factory of Hollywood, armed and guarded by Coca-Cola, Disney, McDonald's and their like, is manifesting a similarly constricting effect on modern thought. For example, there has been a compression of the galaxy of experiences: eating may be limited to McDonald's, or clothing to Nike. There is a reduction in the diversity of language. This process is analogous to the restriction on words – and therefore concepts – in 'Newspeak', which George Orwell introduced in his terrifying novel *1984*.

So how can we win back dignity for citizens as customers? Where is there democracy in the market? Malcolm McIntosh, European director of the Council on Economic Priorities, has described it with supreme elegance:

> Choice. The foundation of a successful market economy. The bedrock of personal citizenship. I shop therefore I am! I choose therefore I have freedom. When I shop I vote. I vote for a certain sort of society, local and global, by choosing organic fair-trade coffee. In making my choice I hope that as an informed member of society I am minimising my environmental impact, contributing to a change in farming practice and significantly aiding economic and social development locally and globally.

What is design all about?

One way to describe 'design' is to call it the achievement of consistent quality and co-ordination of aesthetic considerations as applied to commercial activity. The attention to detail to be found in every aspect of a typical Conran restaurant provides a modern working example of the meaning of design.

In this sense, design is about both the look and feel of a company. Successful designers aspire to improve both the intrinsic character of an organisation and all its manifestations.

Understanding the core, understanding brand values

Brand values are either the conscious or unconscious values that you wish to portray to the world. Usually they are a combination of emotive values and researched business processes. Once established, ideally the brand values should be brought to life in the production of a communication. During that process you should try to make sure that everyone involved with the project understands your brand values.

Commissioning design

To commission design successfully, you need to understand the different types of design. There are two basic kinds:

> ■ **Operational design.** This is about the design of tangible things: your communications, your office, the basics.
>
> ■ **Strategic design.** This is much more intangible: the design of key organisational processes, strategy, the process whereby an organisation discovers its unique purpose in the world, and even how an organisation is structured to achieve its goal.

As a general principle, strategic design should lead the operational design. A very important distinction is the one between output and outcome. It is common to think of design briefs in terms of a preconceived ideas of output. The trick is to try to consider projects in terms of outcome. For example, 'I want a brochure' is a common request from business people. But what is really behind the request may be a different, deeper proposition. Perhaps what the statement really means is, 'I want new customers; I want to operate in a new market', or even 'I am scared'.

When you look at the real issue, you may discover that what is required is a complete redesign of your organisation.

How to brief designers effectively

Following on from the thinking set out above, you should be absolutely clear about what it is *you* want to achieve before you brief your design partner. If you're not sure, follow this three-point plan:

> ■ focus on the outcome
> ■ focus on the outcome
> ■ focus on the outcome

What is a fair price for design services?

This question is difficult to answer. One approach is to use a 'ready reckoner' that suggests that around 10 per cent of the total project cost should be spent on design fees; but really it is more about culture. Think of an analogy to other areas. To what extent does your organisation give priority to design and to what degree does it give priority to financial management? Do you balance the books once a year or develop monthly or weekly reports? Most organisations want some financial management. It is probably a priority; sometimes it is a high priority. At other times it is a maintenance issue. This is similar to the way design works. Is it just about maintenance, or do you want the design equivalent of those monthly or weekly reports?

What are the components of a brand?

We now need to look at how branding consists of a number of components that work together to communicate what your business does and how it can help customers – and do it better than your competitors. Components of a brand include third-party associations suggesting quality or expertise; your business background, history and heritage; your logo and visual identity; and the behaviour of everyone who represents your company, whether in person, in writing or on the telephone.

Some high street brands

First, think about some well-known brands and how they have achieved dominance of our high streets. The great corporate designer Raymond Loewy quoted Shakespeare in his book *Industrial Design* (reissued 1989). In *Hamlet* the Prince utters a five-word comment that typifies everything about design: 'Weary, stale, flat and unprofitable'.

Marks and Spencer

The M&S brand is powerfully plain, almost boasting that, as an organisation, it has the confidence and authority to allow design to be understated. All the signage throughout stores is in one typeface, in capitals. Still today only two logos can be seen anywhere, those of Marks and Spencer itself and of its idiosyncratic consumer facing brand, St Michael. Strict adherence to this austere policy means the company will not even sell cans of Coca-Cola or KitKat bars. This austerity is being gradually updated following disastrous trading results. However, in the past, the corporate reputation for quality and absolute dedication to its maintenance had built immense value for shareholders.

The original idea was that, by promoting all manner of goods under one name, Marks and Spencer could take for itself as profit the huge expense that is normally required to advertise and promote a plethora of premium brands. The main corporate reception area of Marks and Spencer headquarters is a fascinating place. It seems like a cross between a lavish hotel and a state unemployment office. Visitors are forced to queue for the signing-in ritual, under the eye of a doorman. Power and uniqueness are the abiding impressions created.

There is an opportunity cost that results from modern corporate design. While researching this book I visited a number of Marks and Spencer stores. Behind the signs, hidden at the back of one store, was the most glorious set of stained-glass windows. These were of great beauty, but Marks and Spencer had no use for them, because they would dilute the consistent brand expression the store design is intended to create. That is one of the great opportunities that exist for smaller businesses. To use freedom to let the beauty in the world shine through.

McDonald's

One of the McDonald's outlets I have visited actually had the globalisation of McDonald's Corporation as its theme. The restaurant showed large photos of McDonald's branches in cities around the world. Above the till was a huge globe beneath a yellow 'M', and all around were clocks showing the different time zones. Overall, the design scheme was intended to communicate consistency and success, and this is the essential character of the corporate designers' skill. At the entrance to the store, a life-size statue of Ronald McDonald sat, bright in his corporate colours, cross-legged, smiling and clean.

How can you turn this round? What delightful detail from your area could become a motif for your business? Look into history. Everywhere was not always as dull as it is now. Hastings, for example, was the site of a huge battle. What image, perhaps a great painting, could you use at business premises in Hastings, to make people aware, and interested, in where they are, rather than where they are not!

Waterstone's

This leading book retailer uses design well to communicate a thoughtful quality. Dark, almost invisible, cabinets evoke some sense of a luxurious country house, while simultaneously making the product – books – the stars of the show.

Try and follow this philosophy in any business activity. Your business activity is the core of your organisation, so celebrate it. If you are ever in Great Portland Street in London, visit the exclusive bar called Mash. Those great silver machines behind glass at the back of the premises are brewing the beer you are drinking.

Coca-Cola

There is so much to be said about the world's number-one brand. They consistently deliver success through their eminently exportable product. It has been suggested that 'OK' is the best-known word in the world. And 'Coke' is the second. For one example of how Coca-Cola stays ahead, look at their latest drinks-dispensing machines. I recently saw one in a sports shop and was shocked at its enormity and power. Six feet tall, broad, brightly illuminated and clean, with striking imagery, it looked like a spaceship from another world. With a consistent product and advanced refrigeration, these machines seem to offer the opportunity to buy and actually drink from a higher technology.

As a design consultant, I tend to have an instinct about which brands are most desirable to work with: brands such as Sony, British Airways, Mercedes, Intel and the BBC, for instance. Like great universities, such brands attract the best people who manage design brilliantly, which means we can learn the most from them. Coke is still the number-one brand in the world, but is it beautiful? Shakespeare tells us that beauty is in the eye of the beholder, so, given the success of the company, we must probably conclude it is indeed beautiful to many, rather like Kate Moss. But it is a combination of intrinsic design excellence and relentless promotion that makes both Ms Moss and the Coke bottle, beautiful. The Coca-Cola Corporation is also a very long tentacle extending from alien stock exchanges into more than a billion homes. Coca-Cola does take substantial sums of money from most of the world's citizens. That money could go to any local business that provided cold, reliably pleasant drinks.

What is the real secret behind Coke? Consistent delivery. That can be achieved with scale and mechanisation, or perhaps differently, with care. A purveyor of drinks can be consistently friendly, whatever else happens. If you cannot afford a Coca-Cola scale fridge and yours breaks, say to customers, 'I am sorry, the fridge has broken, so drinks are only 5p today.' It might cost you money for a day, but it will be appreciated by customers, and will focus your mind on fixing the fridge.

H&M

Some brands are built on simpler stuff. The clothing retailer H&M, like the men's magazines *GQ* and *FHM*, have decided to put a semi-pornographically expressed sexuality at the heart of their communications. As the saying goes in the newspaper business, sex sells.

You can do this too, in simple and funny ways. For example, if you have an answerphone, or voice mail system, why not try and sound slightly fruity. Don't overdo it but, if you listen to the Orange mobile voice mail system called 'Wildfire', you will understand what I am talking about.

Nike

It is difficult to know where to start describing a brand with the impact of Nike. In sports shops – which are now often just clothes shops – there has been an unprecedented explosion in shoe design. The Nike logo provides a basic theme that is endlessly developed and extended through hundreds of shoe styles. Other shoe manufacturers are also present but Nike tends to buy prime position on the displays. The celebration of gritty sporting heroes in uncompromising photographic poster advertising has given Nike an extraordinary quality. To millions of young people Nike encapsulates a passionate, but intellectually unchallenging, conception of achievement and success. This also draws on our natural desire to display physical excellence, so it is therefore felt by people to be in a basic sense 'true'.

However, to an increasing number of people, Nike also means exploitative 'sweatshops' in low wage economies. If you know where your goods come from, you can make some fun at the expense of a competitor like Nike. All their expenditure on advertising could blow up in their faces if you get it right.

Levi stores

The 'Original' strapline used by Levi expresses the essence of what they want to communicate. The Levi 'feeling' emphasises a synthesised, romantic, emotional history conveying something of the Wild West. Levi do not want to say they are one of the world's largest clothing companies, although they are. Instead, the message is 'think like a cowboy'. Levi stores, sports shops and many other retail outlets often feature TV sets playing videos. The objective is to bring some animation to their visual identities. Videos can also easily and inexpensively be refreshed.

You can borrow this trick, but be less bogged down by the demands of a bland, overarching brand. Any reception or waiting area can, subject to licence restrictions, show old films, or any video that anyone has shot that is entertaining.

Swatch

Faced with national economic catastrophe in the 1970s resulting from Japanese computerised watches threatening to liquidate the Swiss watch business, the brilliant Swatch brand was created. With an eye to the deeper essences of branding and loyalty, the national flag of the small, stylish country of Switzerland is included in the Swatch (a portmanteau word for 'Swiss watch') logo.

Through excellence but not conservatism in design management, Swatch has put Swiss watches back on the map. The Swiss are inventive at building on national associations in product marketing. Near Leicester Square in London is the huge complex, the Swiss Centre, as well as a large sign showing the Swiss flag and the cantons of Switzerland. At many levels, that investment helps all Swiss businesses.

If you are a British business, that is something to be proud of. Be careful here: in our pleasant and mild mannered country, a big Union Jack can sometimes invoke suggestions of National Front or at least right wing sentiments. But what about a symbol from your county? Or what about the words 'Think global, but buy LOCAL'?

Häagen-Dazs

This tremendously successful company has virtually written the rule book in terms of developing and launching a brand. The look and feel of the shops evoke some details of quaint ice-cream shops, but these have been aggregated into a simple retail design. The launch of Häagen-Dazs in the UK combined brilliant PR with unprecedented advertising. The PR campaign involved giving Häagen-Dazs away free at 'society' events such as horse races and exclusive social venues. This created coverage in the glossy magazines that was then leveraged through mass marketing, emphasising the sex appeal of the product.

Highly erotic imagery, combined with brilliant PR made frozen dairy products both high-class and sexy. Naturally the product is very good, but so were the marketing and branding.

Look at the local clubs and associations in your area, and infiltrate them! It is a very bad idea to try and fool people, but you can be quite up-front. If, for example, your local Poetry Society or Golf Club attracts a large number of people who might become your customers, and if you like poetry or golf, join up. Then, as appropriate, if you can afford it, pay for drinks one evening on your company account, but give everyone a leaflet too. They get a free drink, and they remember you. In fact they owe you. You have connected.

Smaller brands in the high street

Generally, retail designs evoke attractive emotions such as those associated with strength, modernity and wildness. This visual language is always building on itself and always evolving. The goods are displayed beautifully, in beautiful lighting, showing off their beautiful colours. A good cosmetics shop is a feast for the eyes and senses. At the more rarefied and expensive end of the market, it is often the case that a modern clothes shop is a gallery of brilliant, bold interior design, and even architecture. The top of the market defines itself through beauty.

This is where smaller business has most often been caught being either negligent or crass. Building a brand is about getting to people in a way that means something to them. That can be done by hiring the most talented designers in the world. Or it can be done by connecting with people in a way that actually means something. To give an extreme example, if your shop plays great music, and people wander in, have a dance, buy something, and dance out, you have beaten everyone. Calvin Klein cannot do that, and nor can Benneton.

Visual identity or 'your logo'

A long time ago I spent many hours arguing with Neil Svensen, the managing director of Rufus Leonard, about the importance, or otherwise, of a company logo. Does the design really matter? This followed from the premise established by Wally Olins on the cover of his landmark book, *Corporate Identity: Making Business Strategy Visible Through Design*, that Neil had just designed.

It seemed to me that you probably cannot make business strategy visible through design. The art of graphic design, particularly of symbols or logos, can communicate perhaps a mood, perhaps an attitude. But a strategy? That would seem to overstate the communications potential of design. Neil agreed and went further. Over time he convinced me of a basic truth.

As a rule of thumb, if you are commissioning new design of a logo, or more widespread evolution of your company's visual appearance, try to follow the following simple steps:

- Don't agonise too much.
- Whatever you end with, use it consistently, everywhere, for ever.

It is the second point that matters more than any other. Remember that your company brand is above all a means for people to recognise and remember who you are. Consistent use of corporate design allows you to make sure customers and potential customers recognise and remember every communication you can make. On the business card you give out with the bill, on the side of your van or building or bags and boxes, in the *Yellow Pages*, basically everywhere, use your logo the same way. That is the key system for building visual consistency, a key component in building a brand.

There are of course circumstances when you might want to change. The best example is the former nuclear reprocessing centre at Windscale, which had so many leaks it renamed itself Sellafield. Or perhaps you have changed your business, or want to make everyone think of you differently. If you have a lot of money, and know what you are doing, go for it. But often the last thing a small, struggling business usually needs is a new logo.

Behind the signs

Together, the components of your brand communicate the essence of your business to everyone who comes into contact with it. If your customers are happy with your products or services, the identity of your business will come to symbolise their satisfaction to them. When discussing branding, words relating to the notion of trust are frequently cited as of great relevance. Many people say brand is above all a promise. The communications guru Marc Sands, formerly marketing Director of ONDigital said in one of my other books, *Beautiful*

Corporations (Financial Times, Prentice Hall, 2000) that, above all, successful marketing and branding are about one simple rule: 'don't lie'.

Underneath these general statements of trust, what is branding really all about? Historically, branding is the combination of a name to describe something, and a symbol to demonstrate or prove something. So a doctor or silversmith might be called Jones but he would also probably want to show he was a member of a notable guild of doctors or silversmiths. Royal crests and pageantry would also help bind groups of people together. The corporate-identity guru Wally Olins stated in his book *Corporate Identity* (Thames and Hudson, 1990) that 'purpose and belonging' are the two main facets of identity.

It may seem odd to talk about the Nazis in a book about branding for small businesses, but some of the big issues mentioned above can be better understood in a large context. We must remember that in all recorded history, Hitler and the Nazis were probably the most hideous and evil murderers. They deserve utter contempt and inspire nothing but despair. So how did they come to power? Germany in the 1920s and 1930s was on its knees. Without any formal position in society, the Nazi organisation provided uniforms for followers and instigated regular marches to raise their visibility. Always wearing the powerful swastika symbol, an ancient Indian motif, their brand was established. In an increasingly anarchic country, they looked organised, they looked ordered, they looked numerous, they looked energetic and they looked new. Their visual identity was frighteningly convincing, and they gained a lot of power and support.

Heritage

Think about this way of communicating with people. What traditions can your company build on? Possible ideas include:

- The first vegetarian restaurant in . . . The vegetarian restaurant Mana in Primrose Hill London proudly displays its first menu on the wall, with prices in pounds, shillings and pence.
- The fastest tyre change in . . . If your people are fast, shout about it.
- As mentioned in . . . Mentioned in books, magazines or on TV. People love almost any kind of fame.

Getting noticed by . . . Using colour, or some other identifier, strongly and consistently. Dyno-Rod in the UK have chosen an almost radioactive version of the colour red to cover their vehicles. They are unmissable! And they have managed almost to make the colour 'theirs'.

Branding and behaviour

People are all very different. We all have different ways of responding to each other. Some people are outgoing, others are shy. Some people seem aggressive, others withdrawn. But, when it comes to running your own business, certain basic principles should be fairly clear. You and your colleagues do not need to be exclusively subservient, or nervous, or paranoid about dealing with the outside world, but a simple fact worth remembering, and even putting on the wall, is simply:

Our customers pay our wages. No customers, no wages.

I was trained in customer services at Harrods, a company who know something about how to treat customers well. Harrods used customer-service training videos from Video Arts, including some great comedy from John Cleese. If you can afford it and believe that your staff need the help, I would highly recommend the Video Arts material. In essence, what Cleese showed so brilliantly was exactly how to get it quite wrong. He showed how easy it is for people to:

- answer a question with another question
- adopt a tone that makes a customer feel foolish
- win an argument but simultaneously lose a customer

The genius of the videos is to demonstrate how quite entertaining and perceptive comments in normal conversation can be very inappropriate and rude within the context of commercial conversation between employee and customer.

The telephone

Your brand is much more than your visual identity, your 'logo'. It is your image in front of your customers. It enables them to remember you and the great service you have provided them with. Your brand is reflected in every form of communication you have with your customers.

Telephones are the primary channel for managing business communications. Email is important, invoices travel by post, deals are done at meetings, but above it all it is the telephone that makes business happen. Business is like an ocean, and we are all deep, deep underwater. Without oxygen, you die, very quickly. And the telephone is our oxygen supply. As a founder and director of a successful design company, I would always make it my business to answer the telephone if it ever got to ring more than four times before being picked up. As the firm grew to fifty people, then one hundred, clients would begin to make fun of me for answering when they called. They used to say, 'Oh, Paul, have you got a new job?' I didn't mind at all. At the annual directors' review meetings I enjoyed stating that my work answering the telephone was part of a culture of attentiveness to telephone answering that was important to the success of our business.

So, after three or four rings, the telephone is everybody's job. Everybody's. If you're the boss or a manager, it is vital that you show you care about the phone. You have to set an example. Try for a moment to put yourself in the mind of the person making the call. When I have been seeking information by telephone it is often because I need to make a preliminary decision, quickly. At this first stage it is often a very small bit of information I need at once, such as:

- Do you deliver?
- Can you send a brochure?
- How much is your cheapest service?
- Can I book you for 20 January?

It is a very good idea to try to make sure everybody who works in your company:

- is prepared to answer the phone
- can be trusted to be polite and sensible
- knows the answer to basic, simple questions

You can spend millions on a beautiful logo, wonderful adverts, spectacular interiors, great products and all the rest – but a single sentence can destroy it all: 'There's no one here now, so you'll have to call back.'

Mind your manners

So here is what in my opinion represents good telephone manners. Start off by saying 'hello' and giving the name of your business and wait to see what they say. If they ask to speak to someone, ask for their name and put them on hold. If the person is there, tell them who is on the line and ask if they want to take the call. If they say no or if nobody is there, return to the caller and say, 'I am sorry, XYZ is out at present. Can I take a message or can somebody else help?' When taking a message always ask for:

- name – check the spelling if unsure
- telephone number – read it back to the caller
- the message – write it legibly

After the call is over, also write your name and the time of the message. Remember, how you act on the telephone means a lot to your brand.

'Brand values'

It is a common maxim that the best brand managers succeed in getting right into the heart of what the brand is about, the 'brand values'. So it has been suggested that McDonald's core brand value is as children's entertainment. Or that Coca-Cola is really about fun. KitKat is the ultimate 'stand-alone' break-time snack. There is some truth in the idea that the meaning of big brands can be reduced to a near ludicrous 'core essence'. One of the joys of smaller businesses is that you do not have to get too concerned about the root meaning of questions that are ridiculously detailed, intolerably bland and essentially meaningless. For example, if you control the Coca-Cola brand worldwide, and their billions of dollars in advertising, and have your own Coca-Cola museum, the question of whether Coke is more about 'fun' or 'refreshment' is meaningful. However, for all but the largest businesses, branding can be a bit more comprehensible and human in scale and detail.

Successful brands are basically about two simple concepts: desirability and consistency. But behind this simple truth comes a more complex idea: are you always going to be desirable by being consistent? For KitKat or Coke, global brands proven in the market place, the answer is probably yes. So if you know your product or service has guaranteed demand, like those of an undertaker or a hairdresser, then the main issue is how best to be in front of the customer to capitalise on their interest. But, if your product or service needs to tempt the impulse buyer, the aspect of consistency that is most relevant to you may rather be innovation. To be constantly innovative will be the key. Can you move customers expectations from 'their hamburgers always taste exactly the same', to 'they are always trying something new'? In my opinion, the latter works where the former fails, so long as you can keep happy trying new things. People often don't like change, at first. But we do love an innovative film, or TV programme, multiple flavours of ice cream or wonderful new books.

But whether you need to be constantly diverse and new, or constantly consistent and safe, the key phrase behind a successful brand is 'satisfaction guaranteed'. One rude comment on the phone or one missed delivery date can ruin a relationship that took years to build. Alternatively, a sincere apology, or fair refund, can turn the same disgruntled customer back to you with increased loyalty.

Conservatism, manners and asphyxiation

As someone who has lived his life in England, I am familiar with, and fond of, some British traits. Our innate conservatism keeps London thankfully free of giant neon signs on top of every building. Our sense of manners can lead people to do things unimagined in other cultures, such as queue. And it is not unknown for loutish-looking youths to give up their seats to older folk on the Underground.

But there is an unfortunate flip side to these characteristics. They can breed a culture where fear of doing the wrong thing turns us all into sheep. The thing about sheep is that they are easy to control. Dogs can do it. Cats and dogs think for themselves but not, it seems, sheep. Big companies are fond of sheep because they can perform the kind of mind-numbing and repetitive tasks that giant organisations are built on. So let us look at two companies' approaches to a fact of life, namely Internet pornography.

A major global merchant bank sacked some staff recently for swapping pornography across company computers. I don't know the exact nature of the material, so cannot say whether they deserved to lose their jobs. However, the police were not involved, so maybe it was not so much a matter of truly evil material as one of taste, manners and policy. This major global bank – which would not think twice about raising a billion dollars for just about anybody to build a factory doing just about anything, anywhere – was forced to act over pictures of naked human bodies designed to titillate.

At the communications company Rufus Leonard, where I have worked for some years, Internet pornography occasionally surfaces to entertain, shock or titillate employees. If some find it disgusting, they will say so. If others do not, they will voice their view. Discussion will break out. Laughter or anger will provoke thought. These sound like human emotions to me. Naturally, if people are not doing their jobs, they should be disciplined, but sacking seems excessive.

It is this rigid sense of what is 'proper' that is the soft underbelly of big business. In a small business, if appropriate, any music can play. The music will add personality to the business. But, with a larger chain, music might upset the 'brand' image that management try to create. So we get a Muzak economy.

What big brands understand so very, very well is how timid and conservative we really are. They give us exactly what we expect every time, and never let us down. They never challenge us, and know how to avoid intimidating us.

How can you compete?

As a smaller business competing against large corporations, think about what opportunities there may be due to the weaknesses inherent in the systems that drive big business. Some of these might be:

■ **Your contribution to diversity and local flavour, your sensitivity to your local market.** Large companies cannot supply local produce or be inventive about how to reach local markets. This would damage their consistent branding. Perhaps people will choose to buy from you because you have more of what they want.

■ **A more personal service and flexibility in what services or products you offer.** Everyone likes to feel important. You won't often meet the boss of Sainsbury's at your local store. Take advantage of being closer to your customers in a smaller business, and listen to what they want. In a smaller business you have the power to change things in response to what your customers say. Big business just can't do that kind of flexibility and personal service.

■ **Flexibility with your staff.** With no remote human-resources department dictating how you must deal with your staff, you can decide how you want them to work, and how to reward them. Maybe they don't want more money, but greater flexibility. Or maybe they want to work all the time and double the size of your business. You are in a position to let them share in the direction of the business if you think they are worth it. No corporation can do that very easily.

■ **Your ability to work with other businesses locally.** Share your customers with complementary local businesses and they will share theirs with you. Together, your network of local business contacts is as strong as the biggest company, and a whole lot more flexible and diverse in your ability to meet customers' needs.

Looking at the 'art' of petrol retailing

Shell has 48,000 petrol stations that all look pretty identical. A battalion of soldiers in plastic armour, looking identical, brightly lit, brightly coloured. Every member of staff trained by patiently researched, tried and tested manuals and guidelines. Whenever I go into a Shell petrol station anywhere in the world, I know what to expect: the same colours and slogans, the same range of products. So, if you own a petrol station, how do you compete? You cannot afford the neon lights, or giant yellow plastic sign costing thousands of pounds. You don't have good supply deals with large distributors of consumer goods. You don't want to light up the whole station all night because of the waste of electricity. And your margins are not so good on many things that you are expected to sell. So what do you do?

Maybe the secret is to put yourself in the mind of the traveller. They are driving at night. They know what to expect from a Shell or Texaco petrol station. Yours may seem a bit more mysterious. But what do they want? Typically a motorist travelling at night may want:

■ petrol
■ a drink
■ cigarettes

- something to eat
- rest
- maps
- friendly company

So why not contact a local hotel and restaurant, and tell them that you can bring them business? Commission a serious sign maker and spend a few thousand if you can. See if you can split the cost between your three businesses. Make a simplified road map of the area and photocopy or print a thousand as cheaply as possible.

Don't worry too much about a logo. Something simple will do: a purple dot or a green square. Anything that catches the eye. Then make your sign read clearly:

PETROL

Food and drink

Restaurant

Hotel

FREE MAPS

When motorists pull in, the first question might be, 'Where's the restaurant and hotel?' So make another prominent but simple sign saying, 'Restaurant 300 yards, hotel 1 mile.' By this point they should really want their free map! And when they buy a can of drink, tank of petrol and sandwich from you, remember to give them the map, which should have cost you less than 0.1p to print. Let's think why the motorist pulled in to visit you. They probably thought of a number of reasons:

- This is not just a pump with someone alone and asleep in the middle of nowhere.
- A free map . . . Hmm, I like free things.
- A restaurant and hotel. Wow! They've got it all.

A final thought. When you have chosen your green square or purple dot as a logo, make sure the hotel and restaurant put one outside, too, to guide your customers. After all, that is what logos are for.

Dress code

I'm not sure that two-piece lounge suits are that wonderful. It's not that there's anything wrong with them specifically, but there is an issue of diversity. This must surely be the only period in all history where every world leader and business person, everywhere, has worn exactly the same type of thing.

It is part of that sheep tendency again. What the media guru Marshall McLuhan said about advertising seems relevant here. He called it 'keeping upset with the Joneses'. The point about building a business is to do something your way. So how should you dress? If you were fixated on two-piece lounge suits as a child, by all means wear them. Sometimes people even expect them. Indeed, it can seem rude to *not* wear them.

My advice, though, is to think hard about this last point. If your business is related to any particular country, why not wear clothes that relate to that country? It may be fun, and certainly memorable. If your business is in information technology, it may already be expected that you dress casually. But what is to stop every industry following the IT example? If you are a lawyer, and confident that you know what you are doing, why not turn up to a meeting dressed smartly perhaps, but not in a suit? Once again, this costs you nothing, and may make a big impression. People may think, Wow! This person is very confident. Or they may think you don't respect them enough as a client and not use you!

Another great thing about this tactic is that it is extremely difficult for large companies to follow your example. But in the end they will have to. So who is leading whom? I firmly believe that suits are a protocol that people are desperate to lose, but don't realise it. I spent years trying to persuade my smarter, younger business partner to wear a suit. And I failed. He won, and I have never looked back. When I used to dress up in my suit it was really an act, and I could be caught out. But now I am just me. You can be you, too. It is as easy as cutting your dry-cleaning bill to nil.

Getting noticed

First you have to tell people what you do, then you have to be different. It can seem like a contradiction, but it is quite often exactly why some businesses succeed while others fail. If you are a printing company it is quite easy to explain what you do. Most types of business are fairly easy to categorise, at least to the people who use them. Harder, perhaps, is defining and communicating the reasons why a customer should give their business to you and not to your competitors. This is sometimes called your unique selling point (USP for short) and is, I think, a useful shorthand to describe this challenge. It acknowledges that most things are alike, directly comparable and basically identical. Of course you can improve design and service endlessly, but, at a basic level, one taxi is like another, one cup of tea is like another, one insurance policy like another.

But consumers often do have preferences – strong ones. These almost emotional relationships to brands are the very essence of business, yet they are the area most often ignored. Here are some examples of USPs that work well for me. Try making a list of your favourite brands. What actually is it that makes you use one product or service over another? Let's examine a few ideas.

Radio 3
The BBC classical channel is in competition with Classic FM. How can they make themselves unique? Think through what their audience do, and how they consume information. I love to read and listen to music on the radio at the same time. It is hard for me to read newspapers and listen to talking. So the decision by Radio 3 to reduce their already infrequent news from three minutes to just one really gets my vote.

The Mash Tun pub in Brighton
It is a reasonably accurate observation to make that all pubs are very similar, passing out the same platitudinous comments in their self-promotion. The Mash Tun tries to be a bit more interesting. It has young and stylish employees, hip music and a good atmosphere. On the pub fascia appear the words, 'Friendly food, tasty bar staff. Groovy ales, real music.'

So these are small jokes but they say two great things. First, we have a sense of humour. Second, we know it is irritating the way pubs describe themselves without any thought at all. It says we are a bit different.

The Great Eastern
This is another delightful pub in Brighton – a pleasant space that feels like someone's house. On the shelves are books, mostly old, odd

titles, probably bought in markets by the boxful, in fact almost value-less. But the impression they create is priceless. Rather than the typi-cal modern pub atmosphere, where every worthless ornament is bolted down against the threat of theft, the Great Eastern feels like someone's house. And needless to say the customers behave far more respectfully as a result.

Glen House

A friend runs a stately home that is rented out to guests for marriages and business functions. Year after year, the same people come back, without advertising or complaint about the bill. What is the key to her success? First, some entertaining details from the history of the building are engagingly woven into conversations, and the website. Second, there is a clever mixture of high-quality service and style, without formality. The result is that the guests get something they could not get anywhere else.

Another important feature of the style of her operation is a certain commitment to quite low security. Guests may find a bottle of whisky in a cupboard without a lock, or some quite valuable vases or pictures it would be easy to steal. But nobody does. Or, if they do take a whisky or two that is not accounted for, what does that cost my friend? Perhaps a pound or two. In the meantime, her guests have been given the impression that they are staying in their own house. What if this policy goes wrong? Well she did once lose a vase worth perhaps £500. But, over ten years, does that really matter? The answer is 'no'. While some regulations are necessary for safety (rules con-cerning possible fire hazards, for instance), over many years, regula-tions, security procedures and other bureaucracy have made us all automata, marching around one another, without looking one another in the eye. Perhaps the biggest opportunity for small business today is just to be a bit more human again.

Automata who are driven more by the requirements of regulation to operate only in certain ways lose the human touch. So don't let the red tape get you down: stand up to it.

Some people hate McDonald's because it is nullifying. It epito-mises monoculturism. Fish and chips are the original fast food, and just as good. Smaller businesses can triumph over great conglomerates such as McDonald's because they are going to make fun of McDonald's. And they are going to remind people ceaselessly and mercilessly. Most importantly, this process will help remind them that they are better than McDonald's. Perhaps they will turn the 'M' of McDonald's upside down and create the 'W' brand meaning 'WE', a global co-operative of fast-food joints that have all signed up to a set of operating principles that guarantee customer quality and integrity in the product, while avoiding pesticides and hormones.

Imagination

By thinking about what bigger companies do well, you can learn about how to increase the value of your brand. You will want to emulate some of the practices of bigger brands, but with limited time and money it is maybe more important to identify what you can do that they can't. I have described what some bigger companies do well and how successful smaller businesses can apply the same methods. But what can you do that bigger brands can't? Think about how your brand can shine through the cracks in the monoliths. How can employing a bit of imagination energise smaller brands?

It is perfectly possible, and quite good fun, to take advantage of what small businesses can do that big ones can't – namely, be a bit light-hearted, perhaps a bit flippant. So why can't big brands do it too? The answer is that they do try, sometimes, but big corporations are normally forced, by either economic circumstances or design, to have to try to appeal to everybody. Many people think that large companies are responsible for a 'fall' in 'standards' and this is in many ways true. They like to use sex and sexuality in advertising, but they have to avoid nudity. Why is that? Wherever large companies employ double standards, they expose themselves to serious competition from innovative, flexible, honest and human smaller businesses.

In any arena, big brands always have to do the following:

- not offend anyone
- seem to be extremely responsible
- seem to be very serious

This last point is perhaps where the greatest potential exists to poke fun at existing brands, and expose some of their lies! It is certainly very clearly true that corporations are not human. Or, if they do have human traits, they are living a bit of a lie. Specifically, by trying to ensure they do not offend, or play about, they separate themselves from the strong emotions and sentiments that make life worth living. And that is exactly where a smaller company can score, big time. In a ridiculous way, big corporations now try to set standards in society. Through their own operations, their bodies, they exemplify behaviour patterns that have emerged as the norms for the industrialised world. These patterns of conduct represent the aggregation of numerous general approximations of appropriate behaviour by managers implementing a series of diverse criteria, including:

- fair (in the West at least)
- nondiscriminatory
- economical
- safe (in the West at least)
- flexible
- effective

What is so interesting about this list is what is missing. There is no mention of any form of meaningful aspiration, ideal, direction or emotional humanity. The corporate takeover of human dignity is depressing and avoidable. As general principles of how smaller companies can act to gain the public's attention, communications or actions can be:

- light-hearted
- sharp
- relevant to our lives

Take advantage of the fact that big corporations tend to be faceless and sprawling, lacking in any humanity. Without losing sight of the lesson of brand consistency that they use so effectively, how can you add some more human purpose to your brand?

CHAPTER THREE

The Relationship between the boss and the brand

Chapter outline

This chapter will look at how branding is about differentiation in forming relationships. Fundamentally this is about having a relationship with the boss. In this sense it is much easier for a smaller business to fulfil what branding is all about: that is, to have a meaningful relationship with the customer.

Entrepreneurs and companies

The word 'company' implies a group of people, keeping the company of each other in whatever they are doing. Companies are made by people, and customers are also people. Behind the fascia and till, behind the gates and the offices, is the drive of one individual, or a small team of people.

A huge framework of law combines with our sophisticated banking and capital market system to deliver the most powerful organisational structure in history, namely the limited company. However, this phenomenal engine of change is started, steered and driven by key individuals, described as entrepreneurs. Many fascinating studies have been made of the entrepreneurial instinct. But it is better to avoid suggesting there is an ideal type of person. If you want to do it, just do it. And those who do it and make it work are it.

Life is quite fixed for us from childhood. We have to go to school, and all have to learn pretty much the same things. At sixteen, the law sets us free. And this is often the age when entrepreneurs will start work. As teenagers we look out on to a world that is very set in its ways. The high street names are familiar wherever you go. Ford make cars, McDonald's make burgers, British Airways fly Boeing planes. The world looks sewn up.

The conventional media – BBC and ITV, *The Times* and the *Sun* – are really rather disempowering. Powerful central editors in each institution gather together and then broadcast and print what they believe we want, and the results are dangerous. Our preoccupations follow a very, very random news agenda brilliantly exposed through Chris Morris's television series *The Day Today*. An atrophied political orthodoxy around institutionalised overconsumption has become ingrained in the industrialised world, without any credible alternatives surfacing into the public consciousness, or the crisis itself even being discussed holistically. Meanwhile, industrial society is now moving at such speed that pollution may actually render our species, and perhaps all life on earth, extinct.

The result of this can be very disempowering. It is easy for young people to feel locked out of a system that has been 'sewn up' by bigger or smarter people and their enterprises. Teenagers look around and wonder how they can best fit in, how they can be of most use to the system. But that is not how an entrepreneur thinks. She will ask how to make best use of the existing systems. She will ask how to make them work for her. Big companies can be seen as dangerous giants, or clumsy dinosaurs, depending on your perception. At heart it is an issue of confidence. Do you have the confidence to do your own thing? The pivotal role of confidence is necessary to achieve the following:

- nerve to risk your own money
- ability to persuade financial backers
- ability to attract colleagues
- ability to win customers

You don't have to be handsome or funny or super-clever, although that helps. No, the key skill is to be confident and thorough. People invest in businesses because they believe in them. If you are a financier, employer or customer, the same rule always applies.

So how does the founder or group of founders communicate their credibility? The first proof is action: to write a plan, show it to people; to conduct research, raise money, spend money – in essence to start. That is the first proof of entrepreneurial fidelity. Anyone who has ever opened a restaurant or nightclub knows the agony of the opening night. Will anybody come?

This is where planning comes in. The rigorous entrepreneur will fill the restaurant or club with friends. First impressions count. So long as you rely on luck, eventually you will lose. Rigorous planning is key. And hard work is the most commonly cited success factor in smaller enterprises.

That said, there is a strong case for working in a way that is 'smarter, not harder'. This principle has been described as the 'stadium effect'. If you are in a crowded stadium and stand up, you will get a better view. But, if your actions cause everyone in the stadium to stand up, no one will be able to see any better than before, and everybody will be less comfortable! So achieving a good work–life balance is not just a good idea personally, but it also makes sense for society. You can be sure that organisations that seek to triumph commercially from the trick of excessive overwork will eventually give off a sufficiently poor impression in some regard or other, and then their customers will eventually abandon them. Hard work can be good, but slave drivers ruin everything for everyone. Reputation is a very fragile and delicate thing.

Think of these stresses and questions in business as analogous to the different types of host who might throw a party. Worst of all is the nervous, overattentive host, who interrupts everyone and becomes the accidental centre of attention just by applying too much hospitality far too often. Worse still, the art of being a host, of making people feel comfortable, is seriously undermined by the communication of excessive anxiousness from host to guest.

Best of all is the calm and genial host. Such a person does not seek attention for its own sake, and wants their guests to feel it is their party. But subtly and effectively such a person will have created all the conditions necessary for a good time. For example they will have advised enough people to turn up at the ideal time. People will actually turn up at that time because the ideal host has a reputation for reliability. And they also have a reputation as a sensible, good person. So the reputation of the host gives some guarantee of the party before it starts.

There is no real difference with a business, any business. Successful smaller businesses are driven by people with the power to build reputations. Don't think that necessarily means you have to be a showy person. It might help, but successful businesses are built over months and years.

The boss and the brand

There are three main approaches to the relationship between the individual entrepreneur and their brand. These can loosely be described as the impersonal, representational and direct. The impersonal are like BP, ICI and General Motors. Key individuals can definitely be identified in the history of these companies, but the modern consumer knows exactly nothing about them. Many business people, rightly or wrongly, choose this approach for small business too. So A.1.1. plumbers may appear first in the Yellow Pages, but who is A.1.1? Or Best Clean dry cleaners, Quick Fix builders and so on?

The second approach, representational, involves a fictional or near fictional identity. Colonel Sanders did, in fact, found Kentucky Fried Chicken, or latterly KFC, after he had entered retirement. But, long after the Colonel had passed on, KFC continued to present his specific human identity as a communications system. At another extreme, Ronald McDonald exists as an entirely fictional character. However, he is consistently portrayed, and understood, as a living person by millions of children worldwide.

Finally, the direct approach involves an actual living person standing directly or indirectly behind an enterprise. The direct model can be extremely anonymous. How many people realised that Amstrad is an acronym for 'Alan Michael Sugar Trading'? Or, at a more direct level, most people know that Richard Branson is the genius behind the Virgin empire. But, if you call up my publisher, Virgin Publishing, and ask to be put through to Richard Branson, you may not be too surprised to find out he's not there. However, his strong and high public profile definitely helps to support the Virgin brand wherever it trades.

It is as if we were following a series of propositions:

 Richard Branson has built a series of successful businesses.
His public profile as a real person helps his businesses to succeed.

- The businesses Richard Branson is involved with are usually called Virgin.
- Because he has built some good businesses, offering good products and services, many potential customers will feel confident about doing business with a Virgin-branded company.
- It is logical to assume that, if Richard Branson is to remain successful, he will seek to ensure that quality standards are maintained at Virgin.

This last point is the one that works the deepest magic. We expect people to deliver on the personal promise of their names. A thousand examples exist, among them a Steven Spielberg film, a Conran restaurant, Philippe Starck design and Paul Newman salad dressing.

In May 2000 I interviewed the brilliant branding guru Steve Howell for an article to appear in the magazine *Marketing Means Business for the CEO*. He observed that the great idea of branding – the concept of promise – is driven far more effectively by a personal relationship with a real person than an amorphous and ill-defined link with an anonymous organisation and its 'brand values'.

A corporate identity can either be conjured up for an enterprise artificially, or expressed in a direct communication from the source. In smaller businesses this can be a great drive for both proprietor and customer. It is usually pleasant to be the person in charge, and many customers can be quite impressed with personal contact. Both parties gain from the exchange.

So the question for a smaller business is: How can you project a personality in marketing that builds your brand? Let's start with a word of warning. Being a successful entrepreneur does not make you a natural TV personality. We have all witnessed very ill-judged appearances on TV or radio by business people who would certainly do better to keep a lower profile. But inside every business person who is successful, or wants to be successful enough to make something happen, there is something or some things that are a distinctive component of what makes that person worth dealing with. In Hampstead in North London, sits Louis Patisserie. In my opinion, Mr Louis makes the best croissant in the world. I have visited his patisserie regularly since I was five years old. Several things strike the long-term visitor to Louis:

> ■ Nothing ever changes at all.
> ■ The pastries on offer are always wonderful.
> ■ It is quite expensive.

Mr Louis is quite prone to parking his Rolls-Royce outside the shop, with its personalised number plate. What is the statement being made by Mr Louis? I have never met Mr Louis, but I have eaten a thousand or more of his croissants. What I know about him is that he owns an electric blue Rolls-Royce Corniche, with gold door handles and a gold *Spirit of Ecstasy* figurine adorning the bonnet.

Either overtly or inadvertently, Mr Louis says the following:

> ■ I am rich and successful.
> ■ People pay me a lot of money.
> ■ There must be a reason.
> ■ Come inside and try my food.
> ■ Find out why!

People complain, perhaps with some justification, about 'fat cats' running the denationalised water and electricity companies. But how many people really object to the wealth of Richard Branson or James Dyson? Such people have gained their wealth by delivering to people what they want.

Stop watching TV

This may seem like a radical thing to say in a book about brand building, and that is as it should be. To build a brand you need to be radical, and you need to be different. Television is a highly passive and immersive medium that turns us into zombies. The culture of so called 'developed' countries is poor indeed, and highly homogenised. In no small measure because people spend an unbelievable amount of time watching TV. According to the AC Nielsen Co. (1998), the average American watches 3 hours and 46 minutes of TV each day (more than 52 days of nonstop TV-watching per year). By age 65 the average American will have spent nearly 9 years glued to the tube.

If you want to understand how devastating passive watching of TV is, and if you want to scare yourself almost witless, follow this simple test. Place your home video camera on top of your TV pointing at the sofa. Just record yourself watching TV for an hour. Next, just try to watch your video for 30 minutes. You will be shocked. You will see how the face collapses, the body slumps, and you become a blank agent for other people's ideas to be beamed into your head. It is wonderful to watch a film or great TV programme occasionally. But, if you really want to get anything substantial done in your life, get away from the TV. It saps your creativity, fills you with other people's ideas and reduces your ability to socialise with others in a meaningful and effective way.

Impersonal?

High-rise housing has failed because it is not to human scale. It does not matter if you have a large space to live in: if the building is fifty times your height, it feels wrong. The same applies to big business: it is just too impersonal. Smaller businesses can offer people the opportunity to live like humans, not ants.

That is something to be proud of. Shout about it. When you make a brochure, or any other communication, don't try to look big. You will fail next to the corporate giants. Instead, go with what you are. Say that your company has grown to be successful by caring about customers, employees and suppliers. It is certainly true that bigger businesses can usually win on price, but they do this by behaving like utter monsters. If you are of human size and scale, let everyone know. If you are small enough to know about what happens across your operation, and care, that could be a key advantage.

People can trust only people. They cannot trust companies, and they know it!

One of the world's largest companies, a company that some say can boast a product in half the households on earth, has tremendous expertise in marketing products to so-called 'primitive' communities. For societies that do not have access to television or radio, a subsidiary of the company uses video vans that reach out into the remotest parts of the world, promoting the company's products.

It is striking and terrifying to think that the phenomenal power and sophistication of technology in the industrialised world is introduced to older, traditional cultures, not through an organised and considered exchange, but through highly commercial mechanisms, designed to lead communities built on cultures based on millennia of learning into our white-hot and completely unsustainable system. Well, this is not some isolated, academic and irrelevant phenomenon. Instead, it represents a commercial opportunity. As the world's industry restructures away from the crassly exploitative big businesses towards smaller, sustainable ones, these case studies in clumsiness will inform consumers that they can really trust only smaller companies.

There are other examples of questionable methods of product marketing. An infamous example relates to Nestlé's promotion of canned baby-milk products to the so-called 'developing countries'. The issue relates to the natural desire for any mother to have what is best for her child. This understandable desire seems to find its fulfilment in the purchase of expensive milk products, so economically 'poor' people spend currency on this baby milk, despite the fact their children would be far better served consuming their mother's naturally produced milk.

So what do these stories convey? If it is legitimate for a giant global business to spend billions of dollars on highly sophisticated, researched and ruthlessly exploitative advertising, it is equally valid for your business, perhaps in conjunction with others, to research into the global operations of your giant competitors, and then undermine consumers' confidence in the acceptability of their activities.

A smaller business that does not have great sprawling global activities is likely to be perceived to be ethically pure. That is such a great advantage to leverage. Let your customers know that you are the safe, responsible alternative. Above all, you must undermine consumers' faith in the idea that cheapest is best. Society has done this once before. We used to use slaves, who worked without human rights, in chains. Eventually our humanity and empathy stopped this barbaric practice.

Now, through the combination of high technology, cheap airfreight and global corporations, we enjoy the fruits of another kind of slavery. This is more remote and therefore seems less barbaric. But it is the same. Great care must be exercised by every consumer to establish that there is not horror at the other end of a product. And only smaller businesses can give that guarantee.

I had the good fortune to meet some people at the Day Chocolate Company, who manufacture the Divine chocolate bar. Some 26,000 cacao (*see* http://www.divinechocolate.com/kuapa.htm) growers collectively own about one-third of the company. What fascinated me was to hear how people at Day Chocolate Company regularly visit the growers and take them examples of the chocolate manufactured. Some people, though I suspect not all, may be surprised to learn that 26,000 people grow a product all year round that they have never tasted – but that is what life is like for a huge proportion of the world's working population.

Big can be silly sometimes

It is certainly true that major companies such as Shell have huge investments in the signs and other illuminated decorations of their service stations. A 7-metre (23-foot) prime sign for a petrol station, even with discounts for mass purchase, can cost $7,000 or more. This is more than many people's houses cost in some countries where the Shell stations stand. There is nothing necessarily wrong with this, except perhaps that it is a grim application of financial strength. Giant seven-metre plastic signs in bright colours, tens of thousands of them, costing $7,000 or more each, represent rather a lot of money.

We can understand how important it is to get motorists to choose one petrol station over another, and the simply vast sums of money involved in persuading them. But there is certainly also a case for trying to channel some energy into gaining a slice of the market. For $1,000, how large could you make a sign that proposed a good car-sharing scheme? Can you make a sign for $1,000 that directs people to a local videoconferencing centre? If you want to know more about how videoconferencing can cut into the hideous cost of fuel, visit www.eye-network.com, the global experts in travel avoidance.

How the system works at present

Remember what Shakespeare said? Beauty is in the eye of the beholder. And so it is exactly with business. As the great Dutch information technology guru and billionaire Eckart Wintzen put it when I interviewed him in 2000, 15 per cent of the economy is food and shelter; 85 per cent is 'fun'. Currently large companies get that money off us through the following system:

 They blast us night and day with billions of pounds' worth of television advertising.

- They operate on a massive national or global scale, crush suppliers and source from wherever labour is cheapest.
- They conduct very heavy consumer research to test propositions with consumers before launching.
- They conduct very heavy consumer research to test the effectiveness of their advertising.
- They hire the best designers, accountants and marketing people in the world.
- They sell us many wonderful things, and a lot of rubbish too.

Let's break down this last point. Which products are sensible, and which ones are crass?

Things that have some significant utility:

- computers with Internet access
- portable stereos
- washing machines
- mobile telephones

Goods that are pumped at us unnecessarily:

- skin products that promise eternal youth
- foods full of fat and sugar to make us unhealthy
- new cars, when our old ones were fine
- endless clothes

Let's take this last point, clothes, and see if we can develop a strategy that gives a business a distinctive 'brand' feel, while addressing some of the problems that occur with the overmanufacture of this essential item. We buy expensive clothes to obtain a new sexual partner, keep the one we have got, scout for a better one, or just for the fun of flirting. Alternatively you may dress well to try to impress your friends, associates or prospective clients – or, indeed, to make yourself feel good. In each case the desire to try to look as good as you can goes very deeply with our species.

So, given that a huge proportion of disposable income goes on clothes to achieve either a conscious or unconscious increase in our attractiveness, how else might this buying of clothes be achieved? One major reason why clothing, even expensive clothing, fails in its purpose, is that it is badly chosen. Because fashions are generally dictated by huge posters and dominating media campaigns, in desperation at choosing the 'wrong' clothes we all shop in the 'safe' high street stores, particularly the ones that advertise very heavily, like GAP. So there is perhaps a latent market based more on clothing selection, than purchase. The clothes you choose to wear, or someone chooses for you, may be more appropriate than those chosen by a remote and careless multinational. This opens up the prospect of centres where clothes can be traded to give more scope for matching the right clothes with the right people.

In essence style is set by fashion leaders in each society. It would shock and disappoint some of the men and women of previous centuries to see how conservative our dress has become in the machine age. The Victorians may have been stuffy, but in Mozart's day, great wigs and flowing robes were everywhere to be seen. Our conservatism today can and should change. In your town or village, it will tend to be a few groups of trendsetters who dictate the style of the rest. Of course we have a lot of prescriptive clothing suggestions sent to us through television, but what the cool young and influential older people wear in any district can be a dominant factor in setting buying patterns. So if you want some of the money that Benneton, Levi, GAP and FCUK are taking out of your area, follow this simple plan:

1 Write a business plan that suggests that a clothing exchange could be developed that would have high standards, be based on matching styles to people, and would boost the local economy.

2 Try to get fifty high-profile supporters of the project to help with the publicity programme, such as the mayor, people who run nightclubs, restaurants, hairdressers' shops and suchlike.

3 Create as big and co-ordinated a splash as possible. Try to make the retail environment very captivating and fun to use. This is a shop where people can get new clothes for old.

4 People tend to fall in love with clothes that they wear for a while, so the business opportunity is to choose the right clothes for them and, if you can do that, they will come to love them.

5 Buying clothes for an average of, say £10, washing them, and selling them – with some personal styling advice – for around £35 would, with sufficient volume, form a great business.

Remember that, to move in this direction, you do not have to start a new business. A modification or development in the strategy of your existing business could work well. The main idea is just to keep looking for examples of where money is being sucked out of your area, and where there is an opportunity to keep it. Satisfying our desire for the new by swapping things more often is a sensible way forward. The art is to learn how to represent old things so they have something of the excitement of new things.

The heart of all businesses along these lines is to make good use of the excessive overmanufacturing that blights our society. It is a huge commercial opportunity for any business that can use local knowledge to co-ordinate more rational and less wasteful consumption.

So much of this task is about building trust, and that is what branding is all about. But this is the trust of a person or small group, earned over time. It is not the faceless aggregation of systems that represents the tragic face of today's giant commercial entities.

Management style

A fundamental guide to the character of any company can be seen in the way the boss, managers and employees refer to the business. If people say 'us', 'we' and 'here', the likelihood is that the business is strong and will do well. However, if people say 'they', 'them' and 'there' you have a problem.

It is not a question of the boss trying to be at work every morning before everyone else, and stay later. There is more to the relationship than that. In fact it can be intimidating and depressing for the boss to have a culture of long-hours machismo. It can stop employees from feeling that they are justifiably pioneering the business in their own way. It is also a rather desperate attempt by the boss to prove to everyone that they have the right to earn so very much more than everyone else. As a leader you have to show, by example, that it is customers money that ultimately runs the business. That may mean staying late sometimes, or all night. Whatever the job demands. But serving some kind of self-imposed prison sentence is ridiculous. Diversity in your life can help your work. Get out of the office sometimes. Learn something about the world, and pass that on to your customers. There is only so much you can learn at your desk.

Perhaps the most striking ratio that you can ever consider, is that between the time spent doing your job, and the time spent deciding what job to do. Not one in one thousand people have got that right.

Incentives

It is the boss who sets the tone of company culture, and decides how the company should be constructed, how it should work. The key to this, the most important component in getting your business to succeed, is to make sure that employees at all levels have proper, material incentives.

People like to feel they're working for themselves, not a boss. Not everyone wants to run their own business, because they don't want the hassle involved in setting it up and maintaining it. So the key to building a working environment where prosperity is the aim of all is to make sure it is in everyone's interest to succeed.

Basics of management, the core of your corporate brand

As we saw earlier, for smaller businesses, the boss and the brand are very difficult to distinguish. For this reason, a poor manager infects a business. They can ruin it. What are some of the ingredients of a good manager?

- fairness
- honesty
- good communication skills
- ability to deal attentively with wages and benefits

And poor managers tend to:

- be inconsistent
- procrastinate
- deal inadequately with wages and benefits issues
- be frequently or generally absent

Avoid these negative traits, accentuate the positive, and your brand will come to positively reflect your good work.

Keeping the right balance

Your colleagues and employees are not necessarily your friends. It can be a great mistake to impose your company inappropriately on co-workers, just because you think that, because you're their manager, they may welcome you. Conversely, at work, you need to be aware that people will think of you as the boss, as someone they may need to turn to in time of crisis.

Strong people make strong companies

I had the good fortune to work with a finance director whom I had interviewed for the position, and he told me the following story.

At his previous company, an electronic-appliance business, he had discovered that one of the salesmen had been stealing money. He confronted the man and he pleaded exceptional circumstances. My friend, called Tim, decided on mature reflection that he would try to help the man. Terms were agreed whereby the money would be paid back weekly, over one year, and the man was dismissed.

Tim then went on to tell me how the former thief, without fail, delivered his weekly payment in cash for a year. I have to say this story bowled me over. Tim had demonstrated such strength of character that it would be a privilege to work with him.

A love of detail is delightful

One of the greatest strengths of the managing director of Rufus Leonard, Neil Svensen, is that he has an uncanny approach to detail and displays methodological conduct in business, generally referred to in the company as 'straight-line thinking'.

Straight-line thinking can be simply summarised as a set of management principles that can be used to effectively regulate conduct in a way that is most beneficial to clients. Some examples:

- Always take action-orientated meeting notes.
- Keep everything in simple files with the subject name printed clearly, in the same typeface, in the same way, on every file.
- When taking a brief from a client, if they say, 'We'll give you examples of our material', after the meeting, approach them again, with a detailed checklist, and methodically work through what you need to collect, ticking boxes as you go.

The net effect of straight-line thinking is the communication of a great sense of competence and order. This is what any customer wants to see from any company. Neat, efficient, ordered, straight-line thinking.

CHAPTER FOUR

Using design

Chapter outline

In this chapter we look at a simple, jargon-free and practical explanation of how design for business works, how big companies do well and how successful smaller businesses apply the same methods. We end with a seven-point test to ensure you are getting it right.

Designing for improvement

When it comes to reviewing and perhaps planning to upgrade and improve your design there are many possible stages and steps you can consider. You'll need to establish a comprehensive programme examining every stage you could reasonably consider as part of a corporate design review. How should you go about it?

Begin by gathering together every single example you can possibly find of your existing design. Photograph any and all of your signs, and stick the pictures on a big board with your letterhead, invoices, business cards, compliment slips, everything. If you have uniforms or other symbols on vans or buildings, photograph them too. If you have packaging, put that up. Everything should be there, every sign of your business.

Try to carry out this exercise for some of your competitors. That need not necessarily mean all your direct competitors, although that is best. You might also include any other business that competes for your customers, and does it particularly well.

Look at your mission statement. What? You mean you don't have one? Well, then, what on earth are you doing in business? But seriously, have a think about how you want your business to develop. Do you want to be number one in your town or city? Or the country? Or is your aim to work the minimum number of hours for the maximum profit? Or are customer smiles the real reason you are in business?

Whatever it is that drives your business, try to write it down. The purpose of the exercise is not to try to communicate exactly what your mission is through design alone, but it can help to judge how you should look against who you want to be.

Set a budget for what you are trying to achieve. It is better to start with what you can afford. Are you going to mortgage the house and get the best international designers, or is your younger brother going to do the work as part of his sixth-form project? These decisions will have to be made. At heart the calculation is about:

- what you are trying to achieve
- what it will cost
- whether the return will justify the expenditure

It may cost some money to get your brand looking as beautiful as it can, but sometimes the biggest risk is *not* taking a risk. And if you completely abandon any attempt to build a consistent visual identity today – because it will cost too much – remember that tomorrow you may have to spend a fortune on advertising to remind your customers that you exist.

Allocating resources

Having set out what you want to achieve and applied a budget to it, you have everything you need to proceed with the project. The next question is whom you are going to call in to help. Graphic-design companies can charge up to a few million pounds to revise a corporate design and produce comprehensive design guidelines. A printer may be able to organise design for 'free', as part of the bill for reprinting. You may decide to steer a middle course, according to your budget. As a general rule of thumb, consider spending at least 10 per cent of project cost on design. So, if new stationery, business cards and a sign will cost £1,000, you should spend £100 or more on your design advice.

That is not enough to pay for even a meeting with an established company, but it may be enough to get some useful work out of a design student. And in an ideal world you could maybe influence their college to help.

But at the other end of the scale, if you have ten vans, five shop fascias and lots of literature, and you know it will cost £20,000 or more to upgrade the lot, then don't scrimp on design. If you're going to do it, do it right. Invite two or more companies to tender. Two thousand pounds is hopefully enough to be taken reasonably seriously. If the designers have good contacts with sign and print people, you could place the whole £20,000 project with them. That should make your life easier, especially if responsibilities are clearly defined.

Managing the project

Maybe you are not a graphic designer. Nor am I. Years in the industry have taught me to shut up and let the experts get on with it. You are an expert on *your* company, whatever that is, and designers should be the experts on design. If you go to a restaurant and fish about in the kitchen barking orders, your meal will not usually be improved. So it is for design.

That said, there are a few issues you could consider that might assist in the smooth running of a design project.

- Does the new design depend on lots of colours, and will that be expensive?
- Can the new design appear in one colour? At low resolution? On newsprint? Do you need a special 'small-use' version of the design, with spiked edges for use on poor quality paper like newspaper?
- What typefaces should be used? Do you have these already installed on the computers that will be used? If not, what will they cost?
- Are there any rules you need to consider for use of background colours? What is the minimum area the new design should have around it?
- Who is going to be responsible for making sure the design always appears consistently, in the same way?
- How are you going to launch your new design? Not at all? In a blaze of publicity? A launch can be good. Think of 'New Labour, New Britain'. People like what is new. However, a word of caution here: if you are having to lay people off, getting the mayor to light up your new sign can be tactless.

Budgeting to maintain the new design

One sure-fire way to ensure you go in for the horrific expense of renewing design too often is to forget to set a budget for maintaining the consistency of what you have created. Keep all the master artwork safe yourself – don't just leave it with a printer who might go bust.

Make sure everyone you work with understands the new design, typefaces, how and where to use them and most importantly why they must always use them.

How to stick in people's heads

Scientists are probably a long way away from unravelling a complete theory of how human consciousness really works. However, some simple principles can be deduced that also help to explain how an aesthetic sensibility develops. Or what makes businesses look attractive.

What can be learned about human consciousness from observation alone? Things happen to us, and we remember some of them, but not others. So how do we decide what to remember? Or how do our minds decide for us? The key that unlocks this process is a change of state. A baby experiences many things, but when hunger agitates an infant, and then the mother provides milk, there is a change of state from agitation to contentment. Experiences at the point of change acquire more durability than those at other times. In this way we learn to recognise our mothers first.

But what do memories do, and how do they interact with consciousness? Consciousness is, broadly speaking, the result of all the senses interacting with each other. It was, for example, Hubel and Weiser who won a Nobel prize for their research demonstrating that cats do not perceive 'vision' in one specific area of their brains. Rather, colour is in one area, shape in another and so on. Many subsequent researchers have substantiated this proposition. It is the constant interaction of these areas that gives us consciousness.

So how do all the memories we have stored interact with consciousness? It is likely that the brain has contrived to ensure that the maximum number of possible memories, perhaps in some selected structure, are put in front of the areas of the brain generating the conscious experience.

Memories may themselves have an active existence away from consciousness. Mice have been shown in experiments to 'relive' the experiences of the day while they sleep. This could be seen as demonstrating that the function of sleep is to provide an 'off-line' system for reviewing, sorting, discarding and filing. It is also likely that memories are in constant flux in the brain, and are perhaps grouping together in constantly shifting patterns. What we clumsily refer to as the subconscious is more accurately 99.999 per cent of what we are at any one time. If this seems like a strange statistic, think of the sheer volume of all your memories, of everything you have ever experienced, combined. These are not with us every second, but they are the bedrock of our minds. Freud was definitely on to something. Although his theories are certainly contentious and perhaps even silly, it was he who began to discuss matters such as human sexuality with openness and intelligence. Through this activity he foisted adulthood on the world, which is quite an achievement

There is, in fact, a great deal of evidence to support the view that memories naturally group together in related families. Any expert, whether taxi driver or atomic scientist is, in some sense, the product of experiences and knowledge aggregating to become a whole mass of connected data. What connects the taxi driver's knowledge of the underlying structure of London is the roads themselves. And what gives a unity to the atomic scientist's thinking is the evolving consensus of interdependent and cross-verified theories, developed over time.

 ## The development of Christian symbolism and visual aesthetics

Although Shell, Exxon and Coca-Cola can all claim to have benefited from the skill of Raymond Loewy as an artist supporting their cause, there are other organisations with longer histories that can claim the support of even more distinguished designers.

The Catholic Church, for example, records its popes back to the first century CE. Designers and artists who have decorated the corporate offices of the Catholic Church include Michelangelo, Raphael and Leonardo da Vinci.

A quick stroll through the Vatican Museum will reveal a kind of glorious, unifying aesthetic, encapsulated in every wobbly detail of every piece. It is a form of impressionism encapsulating a unified aesthetic model of reality which governs thought processes. The aesthetic of the Renaissance was a tool used by an emergent, dominant social and political orthodoxy.

Through the careful manufacture and repetition of forms of visual communication that contain an inherently consistent visual vocabulary – one that differs in a deliberate way from reality as we commonly perceive it through our senses – comes the ultimate politicisation of perception, of thought itself.

What emerged from the Renaissance and beyond was a tradition of art that began to build on a new, emergent aesthetic. The great bulk of both sculpture and painting held by the Catholic Church records particular moments of great consequence in Christian tradition.

Repeated exposure to the conservative, tightly defined visual and aural languages of religious paintings and music has the effect of 'programming' the audience to recognise the family of patterns that comprise the core vocabulary of this aesthetic language.

What is most fascinating about this process of aesthetic education – and we are all exposed to it in one form or another – is that it begins actually to make us see the world a certain way. The common elements in perception of life become strongly influenced by a particular visual aesthetic. It opens particular portholes very wide. It defines our truth. But this visual vocabulary was not summoned out of a vacuum and simply delivered en masse.

It has evolved from a natural vocabulary of shapes, forms and behaviours, and represents an edited, specialist perspective, enhanced and embellished by great artists. In the international bestseller *The Story of Art* (first published in 1950), the art historian Sir Ernst Gombrich refers to these formal traditions as 'patterns' of representation, which were developed by schools of art without regard to the actual visual appearance of things. Traditional Japanese painting uses a lens or 'pattern' of reality to represent the world, rather than simply duplicate it.

There are absolute aesthetic truths locked in nature. We recognise the synthesis of these in art as 'true to reality', valid, real, ordered and beautiful.

Naturally there is also a vast and for most people more important overt language of symbolism and storytelling relating directly to biblical themes contained within these representations.

But my observation is that the essence of the language used by

Renaissance visual artists in religious works is an extension and elaboration of pre-existing visual patterns into an overreaching aesthetic world view. This has the effect of highlighting, validating and reinforcing the underlying reputation of the religious organisation for 'truth' and therefore value through the achievement of beauty. Ironically, this self-fulfilling and self-perpetuating mechanisation of the language of beauty is also self-reinforcing – what the author of *Corporate Identity*, Wally Olins, first described as the invention of tradition.

Art as shaper of thought

Just as some equatorial languages have no word for snow, because the population have never encountered it, so it is with aesthetics. The dominant artistic force controls in many ways the very vocabulary of thought. The power of potential censorship exercised by aesthetic arbiters cannot be overestimated. The design lecturer and artist Anno Mitchell has studied the development of Nazi propaganda in occupied countries in her 1994 research thesis, 'Heroism, masochism and the libidinal economy of National Socialist ethics', and it bears out the point. The first thing the Nazis did after invasion was to take control of the arts policy in subjugated states.

The situation has changed somewhat since the dawn of the era of mass communications. However, it can be argued that Hollywood is manifesting a similarly constricting effect on the breadth of modern thought. And we've already drawn the analogy with 'Newspeak' in George Orwell's *1984*.

Politically, this consequence emanates from the corporate centres of power and wealth in the industrialised world. But the homogenising orthodoxy that blinkers is intrinsic to the excessive amplification of any particular perspective, and results in the huge 'mind share' enjoyed by successful modern brands. Globalisation through corporate capitalist culture has caused this. How smaller businesses respond to it is a key theme of our age.

So much for the theory, but what does this mean in practice? First, there is a robust and simple theory and definition of art as the direct communication or evocation of the living experience. Artists, in painting, sculpture, music or whatever, have a 'feeling', a 'sensation' or sequence of sensations, which they inject into the art they are creating. If – and it is a big if – they are gifted or otherwise successful, they will be able to communicate to their audience some version of how they were feeling. Indeed, the audience will actually feel similar sensations to the artist, as if their minds were joined. As if we were not alone as isolated islands of consciousness, but perhaps joined, by a bedrock beneath the sea.

It is a delightful feeling, whether you get it from the Spice Girls or Mozart, Picasso or Ikea. But what mechanism underpins this basic process? A brief study of the aesthetics of the post-Reformation period reveals that everything, even the artistic expression of individual painters and musicians, is subsumed under the overpowering orthodoxy of a rich and dominant, absorbing tradition.

At a fundamental level in music, tonality was defined like an alphabet, and substantial deviation became an unthinking nonsense. The spell was broken by a very thin, long wedge which laid claim to emotional response beyond the common vocabulary of the classical period: from the first triumphant confrontation of the old order struck by Wagner in the overture to *Tristan and Isolde*, to the appeal by Stravinsky to an ancient order in *The Rite of Spring*, and from there through the searing industrial agony of Shostakovich, to the deconstruction and reconstruction of Shoenberg, leading to contemporary minimalist music with its mechanical lyricism. So, in the visual arts, the impressionists opened an avenue of thinking that Picasso himself developed into an unprecedented city of language in his own image. From that point, as in music, a score of others, including the likes of Jackson Pollock and Mark Rothko, defined their own language for their own emotions, away from the 'tradition'.

Language, as mentioned earlier within the context of Picasso, is the key. What defined the Renaissance aesthetic, so visible, whether in the churches of Prague or the Vatican, was an overarching worship of certain principles of physical tension, in movement, in poise, in the rhythm of bodies on altars, in statues and on canvas. Within the rhythmic tensions and balances of these images, each one pregnant with poise and action, are locked the collective intelligence, world view and political authority of their age.

Sir Ernst Gombrich stated in 1999 on his 90th birthday that market forces have a great role in cultural activity. There is a disconnection at work here. Gombrich describes the effect: 'It is not impossible that there is a kind of inflationary effect. Nowadays you buy a picture postcard at the counter of a gallery which looks very different from the original.'

Look at us now. Do we still have this tension, poise, pregnant action in our art? Perhaps yes, if you look at *Vogue* magazine. But generally no. The aesthetics of the previous generation have broken down, but why? Some suggest that the decline of the empires of Europe holds the key. Essentially this theory asserts that the central feature of an advanced integrated and developed aesthetic is a large group of people who have developed similar tastes, and this advanced sensibility is manifested in the marketplace through more beautiful goods. This mass of aesthetically astute people used to be provided by the 'middle classes', who could, by virtue of a servant class, enjoy the luxury of not having to work, giving them the time, freedom and space to develop advanced and interrelated sensibilities using the collective learning of a tradition.

However, perhaps that statement needs some qualifying. We do have collective sensibilities now, of course. And these are based on the universal success stories of modern marketing and communications, namely Michael Jackson and Coca-Cola, Mercedes and Levi. The key point is, they are not subservient to the slow evolution and exploitation of an established tradition. They are rewarded by evolving new traditions in their own image.

They represent spontaneous islands of order emerging in the chaotic uncertainty of the modern, tradition-free world.

The basic motivations

To get to the heart of the commercial struggle it is useful to consider what basic human functions actually are. They could perhaps be reduced to some basic convergent and the more complex divergent interests. The simple convergent interests are for food, sleep, warmth, procreation and so on.

However, our intelligence reaches beyond these basic instincts into another land, that of divergent interests, of ambition, the lottery of aspiration. This is partly a simple function of attempting to model the future, but it is also the stuff that dreams are made on.

The key component in consciousness is the way it relates to dignity, emotion, creation and so forth. The border between the simple, base pleasures and this infinitely complex land of human potential, be it artistic, humanitarian or scientific, is the border between what big corporations do now, and what smaller business could do.

The great power of brands is to provide certainty. It was John Maynard Keynes who said that money was information about the future. So, in our day, brands aspire to offer similar certainty to help us manage in an uncertain world. But the really big problems, such as climate change, have been caused by the biggest brands. That is the opportunity for the smaller business.

To succeed, smaller businesses need to collaborate, combine and experiment. Above all, smaller businesses and local people need to take more responsibility for the look and feel of the places they inhabit. Remember, if you control how things look, you control how people think. That is why global brands like tower blocks, giant shops and huge signs. And that is why smaller businesses need to work closely with local government planners. Until everywhere looks and feels different from everywhere else, we will be imprisoned by the dreams of remote people.

Design management systems

The challenge of revitalising established brands

I recall being somewhat anxious at the start of my consulting career about my ignorance of the art of brand management. I still know very little – but am now reassured that nobody else knows much, either. So why am I writing a book on the subject? The point here is that there is no great mystery. Brand is just a word. It can have a simple set of meanings relating to the use of advertising, design and marketing. Or it can become a repository for the rehashing of every old and new business theory. The latter is nebulous and mysterious. The former coherent and meaningful. At one level, a brand can represent a whole company. Is the Shell brand related to their logo? Yes. To their petrol station design? Yes again. But what about their pricing policy, or personnel policy, or divisional structure, or exploration expertise?

Shell have described their own brand as the aggregation of numerous business decisions. This is true, but for the sake of simplicity and clarity it is best to study the more overtly customer-facing attributions of brands. In the case studies described later in this chapter, there is one important factor to note, and that is the influence of external market factors. For example, the Apple brand was interesting, and their execution might have been more successful, but for Microsoft. As you'll probably be aware, no single aspect of business dominates the whole. Nevertheless, we can see causal relationships between excellence in brand management, margin and market share.

The minds of auditors have also been greatly taxed by the admission of brand valuations to the balance sheet of some big companies. Company auditors like PriceWaterhouseCoopers patiently examine and certify the exact value of all fixtures, fittings, machinery and other assets that appear on the published Balance Sheet of large companies. But some companies will add some hundreds of millions of pounds in 'brand valuation' to these precise calculations in those same balance sheets. These are invented figures, in a sense, plucked out of the air. Sir Hector Laing reputedly suggested that the McVities' name was worth more than all the factories, fixtures and fittings combined.

So how is great branding done? I asked my colleague Steve Howell, a design director and guru of brand development, about Orange. He commented that Cellnet and Vodaphone were easily handled by Orange, who originally made them sound idiotic: Cellnet, Vodaphone, Dictaphone – these brands were emphasising their technical heritage in a market focused exclusively on consumer aspirations. But have Orange moved on or lost their sparkle? And Vodaphone have now managed to rebrand and look contemporary.

How did they do it? They achieved their goal through consistency in presentation, combined with the art of advertising agencies, design companies and marketers. Consistency is important because people trust what looks together, cohesive and structured. They are suspicious of the ad hoc.

How do companies know when to change?

BT have recently been working to refresh their brand. Their decision to do so was based on a number of factors. First, it had been ten years since the redesign from the yellow 'T' logo to the piper, and ten years is a long time. Fashions for colours and typefaces change. Large companies are influenced by markets and fashions. It is often hard for design consultants to make the case for evolutionary change. But imagine you are driving in unfamiliar countryside. Ahead of you are two petrol stations. An old, dark BP station that has not changed for thirty years and a bright new Shell station. The likelihood is that you will choose the Shell station. People like to believe that they buy petrol on price but this is often a fallacy – the Shell brand, like all other great brands, has never been focused on being the cheapest, but rather the best. A well-illuminated, clean and new service station in an unfamiliar area is worth a lot to insecure travellers.

However, this love of modernity by consumers should not be taken to mean companies should change everything, all the time. Truly brilliant design does not age. The Shell logo introduced to 20,000 petrol stations through Shell International Retail Visual Identity Programme in the mid-1990s was in fact designed in the mid-1970s by Raymond Loewy. However, such symbols are the exception, not the rule.

Evolution and modernisation in design are necessary because consumers have very sophisticated tastes. To give an example, a jeweller's shop window will have a thousand watches, each a tiny variation on the same theme. Yet customers do have a preference. And, although a heritage is generally considered advantageous, in a fast-evolving market, new entrants can come without heritage, shaking up a whole sector with the shock of the new.

Another example of knowing when to change is to be found by looking at the history of Vauxhall. Cars are enmeshed in a market characterised and defined by constant development. The products constantly change; they are on an endless treadmill of refinement. To match the cars, the company has to look contemporary. Although the advertising was quite good, because the brand looked dowdy, in the early 1990s Vauxhall employed the identity consultants Wolff Olins to review their identity. At the start of the project it was clear that the showrooms did not look up to scratch. New entrants such as Daewoo and Lexus were further sharpening the resolve of management to act. Rebranding Vauxhall as Opel or Chevrolet was considered, but eventually an evolution of the core Vauxhall design was implemented. The rather clumsy, block, square logo was simplified, smoothed out and inserted into a round badge. In this way Wolff Olins complimented their work some ten years before updating the ICI logo. A stylish evolution in design can be far more powerful and persuasive than clumsy revolution.

How can managers without design skills decide?

If you are unsure whether your brand would benefit from revitalisation, the simple answer is, if you can afford it, employ experts. And how can you choose a good company? Individuals and consultancies develop track records and portfolios. A manager who is not skilled in design can still be open-minded and interpret design issues in their own language. It is best to avoid looking for magic or a quick fix. Be particularly cautious when you empower individual sales people to develop marketing materials, because certain managers see their prime purpose as bucking against the trend. Such people easily fall prey to designers who lack brand overview and lead to fragmentation in your company image. This is why it is important to get people onboard with the overall design scheme.

A good indicator that something was going wrong could be seen at ICI in the early 1990s. Divisions were becoming bored with being inside ICI, but they still wanted to use the ICI logo. So it began to appear with a rainbow next to it, or some other graphical device peculiar to an individual division. The real message was that the split needed to be done properly, and eventually the separate company, Zeneca, was spun off. It is amusing to note that, before the split, ICI issued the most aggressive-sounding design manual ever written entitled *Code of Practice for Use of ICI Trademarks*. Dispatched with the full authority of the company secretary, it attempted to mandate against wayward designs by reference to law.

Understating revitalisation of a brand is easier in a business-to-business context than for consumer businesses. For example, any company can write to its fifty largest trading partners explaining, 'We have had a serious think about how we're developing and don't be surprised if your next invoice comes from XYZ'. It is a less impassioned more educated audience with fewer strange allegiances. The best drive to revitalise brands comes from common sense and good ideas. For example, it was Thomas Watson of IBM who used the simple expedient of the smart business suit to turn the image of a snake-oil-peddling travelling salesman into something more akin to a modern consultant.

To take the example of Marks and Spencer – a strong candidate for most discussed company of the year 2000 – what went wrong? Essentially they structurally failed to perceive changes in the character of the market. Their St Michael brand's promise of quality and value became meaningless. People now like advertising and are used to much more colour and paraphernalia around purchasing decisions. As our society divides into the wealthy and penniless, quality and value combined become less relevant. All those similar clothes are just not wanted any more.

Branding in banking

In a field where the product is intangible, yet so important, where barriers to entry have fallen away, yet people are still more likely to swap their spouse than their bank, brand managers' energies have been greatly focused. A bank's identity used to be based heavily on tradition, which equated to heritage and security. However, that view changed to 'profit-obsessed' and, as a more business-savvy generation of consumers emerged, new strategies proliferated. Midland developed First Direct, a new channel, but with the funds going into the same pot. Other adventures revolved around the concept of 'softening' brands. Current accounts were launched with names such as 'Orchard'. Yet, as these proliferated, confusion reigned in branches. Few understood what an 'Orchard' account was, and so a backlash opportunity emerged. Innovative banks launched products with simple names such as 'One Account', and the wheel went full circle.

As for the rebranding of Midland by HSBC, the interim retention of the name Midland helps staff acclimatise, but ultimately customers are not very interested. Although the HSBC logo is dated, the exercise of consistent application achieves the goal of communicating size globally. Lloyds faced a variety of challenging issues when merging with TSB. Combining the brands was in the view of one observer a 'business decision'. The advertising, which stated 'together for you', inspired a reaction of, 'Well, they *would* say that, wouldn't they?' But behind the merger of brands one can perceive a simple logic. The Lloyds image was stuffy; TSB seemed to be saying 'small money'. Either would have dated on its own in the current market. Although the combination of a word (Lloyds) and initials (TSB) makes it look as if there were two companies, perhaps – who knows? – the bank may take to using just the horse and either or any name. A masterplan for use of design can and should exist. If you have a clear sense of what you are trying to achieve in branding terms over the long term, you can ensure that each modification and development is leading your organisation towards an ultimate goal.

Who does it well?

Many communications professionals admire Xerox's success in positioning themselves as 'the document company'. Other successful newcomers include Lucent Technology, a division de-merged from tele-coms giant AT&T. Because nobody had heard of Lucent when it was launched, AT&T included mention of 'Bell Labs' in the name. In the US Bell Labs were famous for world-changing inventions such as the transistor, so, by saying on the launch advertising and business cards 'Lucent, incorporating Bell Labs', the new company cleverly linked the rich heritage of Bell Labs to the excitement of a new enterprise. Although neither Xerox nor Lucent has performed brilliantly in recent years, it is difficult to blame branding for the problem. Image-wise, these companies were strong. Poor branding can be seen in companies like the French IT giant Groupe Bull, whose tree-grid logo is terribly laboured. Brands die, Rover will probably die, and few will mourn it. Of course unemployed workers will feel the pain, but what consumers mourn BOAC, PanAm or British Leyland? Consumers do not care about giant, anonymous companies, and the feeling is mutual. Some brands are quite bizarre. Of course, you do not think of actual beetles when you hear of the Beatles, and the same goes with the Rolling Stones, but Radio Rentals is ridiculous. They don't rent radios!

What of British Airways?

As with the fate of M&S, the British Airways identity has become a topic of popular discussion. Although commentators have criticised the recent redesign – when the Union Flag motif on the tails was replaced by an 'ethnic' device – for betraying a uniquely British iden-tity, there was only an abstract quarter-flag before the revamp.

Commentators have criticised Robert Ayling (sacked as BA's chief executive in March 2000 after four years at the helm) as having been rather brutal to staff, and this sat badly alongside a flamboyant approach to plane livery. Combined with jingoistic tabloids and polit-ical interference, this resulted in a fatal lack of nerve. The decision to abandon the big idea of 'diversity' behind the design programme, and replace it with hackneyed Union Jack ribbons may seem incidental to the company's decline, but it is worth remembering that Bob Ayling lost his job anyway, even though he tried to appease tabloid opinion. Homogenisation is dead and I admire BA for trying to project that fact in design. In my view they should have pressed on with it.

Brands built around strong individuals can communicate their company's character and essential ideas more quickly. They seem less like the big 'I am'. If Marks and Spencer could get people like them, that would be clever. Sainsbury's positioning was good. The advertising was great, and employing contemporary architects and so forth should have been a recipe for success. But marketing messages come unstuck if they are not matched at street level, and many Sainsbury stores were dowdy.

Brands on the Internet

The final piece of the jigsaw is actually the door to a new puzzle. People should no longer be asking, 'Have you seen so-and-so's website?' People should get what they expect from brands online. For a car company this would mean pictures, details of colours available, performance statistics, comparisons with competitors, and perhaps how to get a test drive. Be prepared to seize the opportunity. The eminent management consultant Peter Drucker has observed: 'Traditional multinationals will in time be killed by "e-commerce".'

Lessons from experts in design

A large company once commented on how its design management department was increasingly concerning itself with areas beyond simple visual appearance. For example, while making sure that a coffee cup used by customers bore the company mark in the correct colours and position, the department also considers whether it can be stored easily and used comfortably, whether it is durable and so on. In this way, design management becomes a form of total-quality management, an approach that smaller businesses can learn from.

In terms of achieving consistency, just getting a handle on the problem is half the battle. The design manager of BT described his approach in 1993:

> When I was offered the job, my first action was to undertake a large visual review involving hundreds of photographs. I photographed everything and said to the chairman, 'I can sort all this out for you but I will need two things: firstly a lot of money and secondly the full support of the board.'

Tone of voice in the mechanical industries

In the early 1990s I interviewed the design managers of three privatised utilities. They described their companies as 'engineering-based'. This meant that corporate communications bore a heavy technical emphasis in the writing style. It needed to be reworked to give it more 'customer-orientated' language. The production of 'guidelines' relating to writing style is a possible solution to this problem, and it is a great way to build consistent brand identity, even for a smaller business.

Why does a large company want to redesign its logo?

In an in-depth seminar programme during 1992 and 1993 I researched many of these issues with leading Britsh Public companies. To ensure candid and comprehensive responses it was necessary to maintain some annonymity, and this is reflected in the following case studies. A big finance house once commented that the chairman had been very dissatisfied with the extreme diversity of publications. It was felt that they looked as though they came not from one company but several. A major corporate-identity review was launched, and the Corporate Communications Department was expanded to cope with the extra workload. Result (among other things): a logo that was identifiable throughout all the company's communications.

Names and logos that reinforce each other

It is worth noting that the Eagle Star symbol has one of the greatest possible strengths of any identity design: the logo as a visual representation of the name. This similarly applies to Shell, Orange, Goldfish and Blue Circle. It is perhaps not surprising that Eagle Star have one of the highest recognition records of company name, from the logo alone, of any insurance company.

Historic loyalty

The acquisition of a business will normally result in a potential demoralisation of staff. There is a natural reduction in entrepreneurial, frontier spirit, even though proprietors who sell their businesses tend to receive excellent financial rewards. To mitigate this negativity, in design terms, there seems no reason to force the fact of new ownership down employees' throats.

The delicate way to handle acquisitions is over a period of time, with the new holding company logo beginning to appear on stationery, literature, vehicles, and so forth. Alternatively, if the whole point of the exercise is to make a bigger splash, and people from both companies feel positive about that fact, maybe it is good to spend some money and make a big impression from day one. When Coral bingo merged with Granada, to form Gala, they did it at one stroke with a big splash.

Why consistency is easy for some and hard for others

Established companies that have long been in existence, without much change, find it easier to project a unified identity. Companies that have grown by merger and acquisition express the view that they are, in reality, a variety of distinctly different businesses or separate companies, grouped together under one name. This fact makes the task of projecting a unified identity particularly difficult.

Different attitudes to partnership or association

Different companies owned by bigger companies have different attitudes to the potential value of parent-company endorsement. Some are pleased to show they are backed by international resources, whereas others have developed a policy on endorsement and still others are keen not to be associated with their parents.

To give an example, a privatised utility that had purchased businesses outside its core operations was selective with regard to applying the corporate identity to acquisitions. For a business providing basic maintenance to households, endorsement from a reputable, established public company is considered to be of great value. Conversely, if a subsidiary manufactures consumer goods such as food, association with a utility is probably unappetising.

Logo pitfalls

Extensive on-site testing of any potential design can help avoid trouble later. However, some problems will inevitably arise. For example, a mark that looks like an arrow can be confused with a directional symbol, making it difficult or inappropriate to use on signage.

The importance of communication

A design manager in a larger business put this issue well as follows:

> Awareness of design and identity has to be cascaded throughout the business. Communication is 90 per cent of the problem. Most importantly, however, the cascade of information must have the force of 'law' — it must have the chairman's signature.

> We are trying to build up a culture that is design-aware. We are
> holding courses with middle managers in literature design.

Advice on launching a new design

This piece of advice is from an anonymous expert . . .

> Regarding a launch, if you want to attract criticism, you want to
> do a big public launch. Our identity was evolutionary, not
> revolutionary. Naturally we did spend some time to make sure
> that all staff, sales people, franchise holders and other
> intermediaries had some idea of the purpose of the exercise, but
> overall it was fairly low-key.

Building a culture of excellence in design

To make everybody in your company understand the importance of
quality design in communications, it is important to show how things
are done well. You must not be negative with colleagues but positive.
The ultimate sanction that the boss may have to ensure quality of
design is withdrawal of authority to use the logo, effectively
paralysing the operations of any area that has this sanction –
described as the 'atom bomb' – enforced.

To some people in companies, design is like plumbing or accounting: a basic function to be dealt with, not celebrated. This is wrong.
Great design can redeem anything. In a battlefield, at the darkest
moment, troops will often raise their national flag. Why? Because the
symbols we use to describe what we do are potent representations of
what we are. Your company design is not a dull detail, but your face.
What company would be willingly ugly? That spells commercial suicide.

Does your logo have a name?

It has been suggested that it is much easier to discuss corporate design
on a regular basis if the corporate 'symbol' or 'mark' has a name. It
might be called the arrow, roundel, 'C' sign or whatever, but it should
have a commonly accepted name. It is also useful to have a central
register of everywhere it appears. You can use this regularly to check
the cleanliness and general quality of all your signs.

Project assessment

The correct approach to a design project is difficult to ascertain. It
may be appropriate to assess the job against various criteria: Is it for

an internal or external audience? Is it for the whole company or just a branch? By establishing the project's position within a design 'matrix', it may be easier to approach it with the right budget, systems and emphasis.

Livery

Experience suggests that the only way to discover what will go wrong in the application of a new design scheme to vehicles is to run a test with the real thing. No amount of research can compare to the practical experience gained from applying new livery to a car, lorry or delivery bike.

Substandard logos

Those people in an organisation who generate literature must be discouraged from using substandard versions of the logo. A common fault involves the use of poor computer scans (low definition or taken from a low-quality original), instead of a master artwork. It seems sensible for managers to send high-quality electronic versions of the logo to all who use it across the company. However, this requires a full knowledge of the computer systems and software in use.

What's in the system?

A major advantage of a thorough approach to design involves a review of computer systems for literature production within the context of their actual use. In this way a design-aware manager can drastically reduce the variety of forms and other stationery in circulation across a business, thereby avoiding overstocking and duplication. Such an approach will also highlight the need for computer compatibility as an operational imperative as well as for technical convenience.

Information overload

A good, design-aware manager will be careful to avoid the existence of too much promotional material. Sometimes it is possible to send interested parties some twenty or thirty brochures about your company, but not one that summarises the whole organisation.

Looking smart

One very experienced design manager has commented on a powerful way to avoid what Wally Olins has referred to as the 'Sellotape' culture. 'To help make the whole place look smarter I have scrapped thousands of notice boards, and replaced them with lockable notice boards'. Why does someone do that? The answer is clearly to avoid people putting horrible signs up.

Another manager has described to me the exasperation involved in trying to build common visual standards among colleagues: 'We cannot get operatives to wear safety gear, let alone uniforms. Trying to get people to follow grooming and clothing guidelines is extremely hard. A major element in the new identity has been getting the culture through to employees. We are always talking to them about quality of service.'

A positive system for mitigating this problem is to incorporate it into training. Company induction is important. New people need to be told about your company's aspirations rather than the company's depths!

Design buying policy

Most companies have a central system for buying print or organising web pages, and this is useful. If your colleagues are permitted to use only an approved design supplier, and even perhaps if they must always seek permission from you before purchasing design, then it becomes easy to exercise central control. It is very hard to use the wrong typeface if it is not on your system. So, to achieve a consistent look for your business, you can remove all but your approved corporate typefaces from all computers and printers.

Summary – and seven key tests

To summarise, bearing in mind that good corporate brand management is vital to the success of your communications programme, ensure that it doesn't qualify as:

- unglamorous
- underresourced
- Not RECOGNISED

And let us end with seven key tests for sound brand-management practice:

- Is your brand considered an asset?
- Is it consistently applied?
- Do you know what is happening?
- Are you consulted?
- Do you have an annual plan?
- Are you considered as a resource or an obstacle?
- Do you feel your brand is working?

CHAPTER FIVE

Thinking about your customers' experience

Chapter outline

*In this chapter we try to get into the mind of the customer, and how he
or she looks at you. We look at your company from the customer's experience. Do you, for instance, have a comfortable place for customers to
wait? When you visit customers' premises, do you strive to leave them as
clean as – or maybe even cleaner than – when you arrived?*

How well do you know your customers?

In order to get business right, you need to try to see your company
from the customer's point of view; you need to understand your customer's experience fully. From this understanding you can discover
what it is that they like about your business, and build on this.
Equally, you can maybe spot some minor irritations that wouldn't
cost much to fix, but would make your customers feel good about
your business.

Many enterprises are seriously lacking in their understanding of
customer characteristics, behaviour and preferences. They therefore
risk failing to make the most of each interaction and thereby open the
door to the competition. You need to try to have a deep understanding of who your customers really are, what motivates them and why
they would choose to do business with you.

You can pay too much attention to how and why customers

purchase, and too little to how to maintain effective customer relations *after* they have bought from you. A customer is worth a lot of sales. Enterprises that are truly concerned with keeping their most valuable customers will try to identify customer needs at each stage of their interactions, for example:

- product information
- ordering process
- delivery
- payment
- support

Think about the different stages you go through when selling your product to a customer. At each stage, they interact with your business. Ask yourself whom they would be dealing with, and whether that would be on the telephone, by email, letter or a meeting. Can you improve anything for your customers at any stage? Does the way each stage is handled reflect your business as you would like to be seen and understood?

You will likely find that, at each stage of contact, your customers have different needs, and you may have different ways of interacting with them throughout the process. The needs and experience of your customers may relate to the reasons they are purchasing from you, and the choice available to them in the market at that time. Give them a better experience than they will get elsewhere, then they may just come back again and again and again.

The formal study of customer relationships is often called customer relationship management, or CRM. Big business often has CRM processes and technology solutions. In *CRM Magazine* of October 2000, Melinda Nykamp and Carol Rozwell write:

> Tapping into the potential of customer interaction information is one of the essential components of successful CRM initiatives. Experience shows that customers make the decision to do business with one organization over another based on more than just product or price – they make their decisions based on their overall experience, which includes sales, service, recognition and support. Organisations with successful CRM initiatives realise that customer retention involves getting it right, not just on the first interaction, but on an ongoing basis.

So the message is:

> ■ Keep listening to your customers.
> ■ Know what your customer values about doing business with you and keep delivering on it.
> ■ Be alert to the different requirements that your customer may have at different stages of the sales cycle.

For customers, feeling good about doing business with you will often go far beyond the features and benefits of the particular product or service they are buying. Customers will feel good when their interaction with your business is enriching, and when they are pleased that they have spent their time with you. Businesses that make us feel good are the ones we trust, and building trust is a massive element in building your brand.

Creating a valuable customer experience

What is appropriate?

Your interaction with your customer should be appropriate to the level at which they are doing business with you. The customer should be happy with the media used. For instance, do you need to have a meeting when the customer's needs can be met on the telephone, saving everyone's time? Would your customer rather not be interrupted? Could you use email for this interaction? Is it best for you to go to see your customer, or is there a benefit in their coming to see you?

Your customers must feel they have control. If you listen to them carefully you can match the ideal experience for them. Try to eliminate any possible interruptions in the flow of their experience, unless they choose this. If they want space, give them space. Otherwise, stay in touch meticulously. If you use any kind of technology to manage your relationship, keep it invisible if you can. To give an example, Amazon.com are very good at suggesting books to customers based on their previous choices. But Amazon do not say, 'We have profiled you as a member of these three group categories and as a personality type 7', they simply say, 'Would you be be interested in this book?'

Stimulate your customers. Make your relationship interesting and they will want more of it. How can you appeal to their minds, senses and emotions to produce a positive experience for them? Have fun with your customers. Make business pleasurable.

Orange, the mobile-phone company, has a certain style I admire. There is a consistency of approach and a clarity to its communications that allow it to occupy a distinct, satisfactory and reassuring place in my mind. A good illustration is that, when you leave a message on an Orange phone, a delightful voice has asked you to do so. It is the only mobile-phone company that seems to have a personality beyond the computer. It is intangible, and that is what's interesting. It gives me some confidence in the Orange brand. Someone has thought deeply about the customer experience.

Keep developing your relationship, because it gets more and more valuable over time. Finally, are your efforts consistent and appropriate throughout your customer's relationship with your business? 'Getting on the telephone' is the standard mechanism whereby many in the City of London make money.

Using the right tone of voice

People are becoming less stuffy, and that is a good thing. When people in business call me Mr Dickinson, I find that weird, and slightly disturbing. Being called Paul feels right for business transactions. But a word of caution here. Never confuse informality with rudeness. It is good to be called Paul, but never 'son' or 'pal', as these are over-friendly, perhaps even slightly annoying, epithets.

Doing the right thing

In the normal language of business, a valuable customer experience is one that makes a consumer want to do repeat business, and delivers monetary advantage to a company. And that is as far as the words can be stretched. But my dictionary describes experience as including feeling, and accumulated knowledge of practical matters. As stated earlier, despite the giant neon signs and huge plastic interiors, global business is not practical by any stretch of the imagination. It uses a veneer of anonymity to disguise its impracticality. But you do not have to dig very deep to reveal the rot.

To give an example, it is amazing but true that 80 per cent of waste products come from industry, a figure that makes domestic waste look fairly irrelevant. It is puzzling how companies, which comprise individuals, many of whom have children, often act in a way that is threatening to their children's lives. Think how you can develop your customer experience to embrace something more than the petty, banal provision of endless excessive goods and services. Fight the vapid and irrelevant, and deliver a really meaningful user experience to your customers. Edward Wilson of Harvard University calls this confusion of endless choice 'discontent with superabundance'. But that is only because we have too much irrelevant, thoughtless products, and not enough thoughtful and sustainable ones. By thinking deeper about the needs and responsibilities of people, you can win market share, and margin.

Broadening out what business is about

When I interviewed him for my book *Beautiful Corporations* in 1999, Jamie Anley, a founder of the brilliant and innovative design consultancy Jam (www.jamdesign.co.uk) said, 'In our society an artist may respond to a work of art, but a business person may not.' This simplistic statement is a real area of potential difficulty. Those companies that can liberate the potential of their staff's intelligence will prosper. The true danger comes when the corporation and the consumer forget they are one. Everyone in a corporation is a consumer. But, when corporations forget they are part of consumerism, the consequences are frightening.

Jamie has been interviewed by the web design magazine www.sputnik.ac, where he elaborated well on this point: 'We [at Jam design] say a company's brand image is made up of two things. What they do inside and how they communicate themselves outside. If these two become one it becomes a very strong brand. Nike is a cool brand, but then people found out that they use children to make their shoes! Their external image has become so far removed from the company they are on the inside it was bound to lead to trouble.

'Conflict often starts when people hit brick walls and don't see any way out. That's when people go crazy. And this is what will happen to many industries unless they change their perception. Ten years ago, we would buy something based on price. Now we make decisions based on emotions like . . . "Do you pollute this planet?" or "Do you treat children badly?". We have more access to information via the Internet, which has made a lot of corporations weaker. For so long they thought they were outside of society.

'You get people who at home are serious eco freaks and when they go to work they spend all day polluting a river - they separate their work from everyday life. It can't happen any more. People have to see that it's all one planet.'

In their work for Sony, Philips, Evian, DuPont and Whirlpool, JAM have looked deep into the products companies make, and discovered their essence, their cultural currency. JAM then recycles this learning into brand development.

Genius marketing

If you are challenging perceptions, you are making the story. The marketing budget for NASA to send a rocket to the moon is zero. The act is so fantastic that all the world's media will engage full boosters to get there without any need of hype. If you are involved with something progressive and exciting, people will want to know about it. That is what the media are there for.

Although anyone with money can buy commercials and bigger companies have impressive budgets, they can sometimes demonstrate very poor organisation. They are so large that the tremendous excitement and innovation that are generated in the design division at global headquarters do not manage to spread out to the different regions and divisions. That is where smaller businesses can score.

The case against market research

You cannot study the past to reveal the future. Any company that decides to use market research to anticipate where people are going, and then tries to develop a strategy around this information, will be forced into the expensive process of following trends. Truly innovative business people should not be looking outwards at what consumers are doing, but rather looking inwards at the company's core, and thinking about how it can be most creative with those resources. Research almost contradicts the idea of development.

Corporate punishment

Giant companies are truly horrific organisations. As David Korten explains in *When Corporations Rule The World*, General Motors' 1992 sales revenue roughly matches the GNP of nine countries with 550 million inhabitants, or a tenth of the world's population.' He fears that, 'Unlike real people ... corporations are able to grow[,] ... amassing power indefinitely. Eventually that power evolves beyond the ability of any mere human to control.' He also quotes the political embodiment of apple pie, President Abraham Lincoln, who observed just before his death: 'Corporations have been enthroned ... An era of corruption in high places will follow and the money power will endeavour to prolong its reign by working on the prejudices of the people ... until wealth is aggregated in a few hands ... and the Republic is destroyed.'

The statistics are terrifying. Wal-Mart Corporation of the USA has annual sales of over $150 billion, more than the GNP of Poland and Greece combined. Microsoft Corporation has had a market capitalisation of more than $500 billion. Contrast these figures with, for example, the UN estimation of $9 billion as the cost of providing safe drinking water for the 1.3 billion people who suffer without it. And what is the point of this diatribe? It is that our world has gone completely mad. Consumers are being absorbed like tiny particles of water by the giant sponge of global capitalism. Smaller businesses that can communicate to consumers that they are pro-life will succeed. How many times have you heard people say they went on a brilliant holiday to somewhere that was 'completely unspoiled'. Big business can ultimately only spoil, but smaller businesses can cure the future by bringing back some of the diversity, richness and complexity of the past.

Developing and understanding corporate values

It may seem ridiculous to think that an organisation could be materially affected by its values, but that is just how countries work. 'Life, liberty and the pursuit of happiness' defines some key aspects of the American experience. The spirit of 'liberty, equality and fraternity' can partially be seen in France. However, the cosy aspirations of those pioneers who framed constitutions are sometimes distant from contemporary realities. In business it can be that people actually 'live' the corporate brand values to a ridiculous extent. To optimise personal performance, managers need to keep an eye on reality.

The art is to achieve the optimal alignment of marketing promise and operational capability. It is the degree to which you can insinuate your company into the customer's mind and then whether you can deliver on that promise.

An example of this principle in action is that of hotels. They are one of the principal environments in which an embracing, positive experience needs to be created – and style clearly creates value. The great identity consultant Michael Wolff, who was co-founder of Wolff Olins before leaving in the mid-1980s, wrote a short booklet many years ago with the idiosyncratic title *You Are a Towel*, to draw attention to the powerful role such details have in the perception of customers.

Style in business

The expression of style is about individuality and personality. All the best companies have it. Style is not neutral: it is a great motivator of people. Whatever you buy in business is just a promise; but, if that promise has style to it, that style makes it powerful.

In the high street there is more style than there used to be. Years ago shops would do things pretty much in their own way: their businesses were 'thrown together', without much care. After World War Two, people simply did not have the money to be stylish. Now every shop has a defined identity. But, because this has been achieved by multiple retailers, every high street looks the same, so we have lost some of the individual style of yesteryear, and that is a huge commercial opportunity.

Today's corporate style emerges from market research and focus groups. This means that modern brands are incredibly powerful and well thought through, far more so than twenty or thirty years ago. However, they are not particularly exciting. Years ago, leading-edge retailers such as Heal's represented style. Style was present in exciting 'pockets', here and there. But bigger businesses have crushed that diversity. Only smaller businesses with a plucky character can bring it back.

Using the medium you own to build your brand

When discussing the development of this book a colleague said to me, 'What about some company that is intrinsically dull, like a cardboard-box manufacturer? How can they make their brand bigger?' The answer is simple. Look at what you do as the agency for raising your profile. In the example of the cardboard-box manufacturer, I suggested putting famous poems on the sides of boxes. There are many reasons for doing this:

- It would cost very little.
- Most famous poems are out of copyright.
- Poetry is a wonderful thing that few people consider.

Overall, through this process, the plain old cardboard box can become capable of creating laughter, or tears; it can move the heart, uplift the soul. And, throughout this process, the brand of the box manufacturer rises and rises in significance.

Get Mozart and Michelangelo working for you

There are many other great works of art that are neglected in our society. Classical music, painting and literature are generally copyright-free. For music, there may be rights owned by performers, but a simple investigation of copyright law reveals that the great mass of the world's culture is freely available for you to pass on to whomever you choose, for no charge.

If you run any kind of facility that people attend, it can be that softly played and well-chosen classical music will increase the pleasure people extract from using your company. But be aware of the importance of choosing the right pieces. The symphonies of Beethoven are marvellous pieces of music, but they can be very stirring and therefore distracting, and will sound awful piped into a waiting area. Some classical music is imposing, and it can jar and shock the listener. So choose well.

Gentle pieces from Corelli or Mozart should work well, but be careful to listen to them all the way through. Spend time at the weekend familiarising yourself with music, ideally by listening to BBC Radio 3 or Classic FM. They will always tell you the names of pieces, so, when you hear something delightful and relaxing, write down the name.

As for paintings, it is extraordinary the degree to which companies spend time and significant amounts of money printing dull and forgettable brochures. If you are going to produce something in colour, be it a letterhead or brochure, do you have room to reprint a painting by Rembrandt, Degas or Picasso? In black and white you can reprint the drawings of Michelangelo. Wherever there is a commercial communication, there is simultaneously the opportunity for art to be used to increase the pleasure of the consumer's experience, and to grow the power of your brand.

Comfortable, cosy and clean?

It is very good to keep business premises clean. It is often said that you can tell how good mechanics are by how clean they keep their garages, and there is some truth in this. When people see that your premises, products or vehicles are clean, it shows you care about things. And care is what counts, and what makes people buy.

At the extreme, you can get some quite bizarre situations. In 1999 I visited the headquarters of the giant US computer companies Oracle, 3Com and Cisco. The last one was the most powerful. What seemed like hundreds of near-identical Cisco buildings stretched either side of a great boulevard. And each one was almost impossibly clean inside. This makes the customer or anyone else visiting Cisco feel respected, important and valued. It is even slightly intimidating, and yet, ironically, it can help to make you relax because the environment is unambiguous, providing a rather clinical and formal environment where business is the order of the day. This is why I usually avoid staying at bed-and-breakfasts, because they often feel more like somebody's home that you are invading than a hotel.

Now it is very hard for a small business to compete with a company such as Cisco for cleanliness. You have to spend millions on either new buildings or endless redecoration of old ones – plus paying a monumental cleaning bill.

So what can you do? The answer is to try to make your working environment, for both customers and staff, a bit more comfortable. First, don't necessarily trust your own taste – but can you think of whose eye you do admire? Ask around. Do you have a friend who can advise, or a local shop that is particularly beautifully designed? An expensive hairdresser or fashion boutique will often present a good example of how a few objects, perhaps a carpet or coloured light, a bunch of flowers or big bold mirror, can transform any environment.

Take advice from someone who everyone agrees has a good sense for design. If you can manage to build an environment where style helps to define your brand experience, you will be able to achieve something that big companies can never do. A big company is a mass of compromises made by hundreds of people into a kind of corporate consensus. This is usually quite smart and businesslike, but desperately dull! A smaller business can build a bigger brand by building comfortable, stylish and cosy environments. How many bank branches can you remember the inside of?

Taking care to communicate well

It is vital that companies communicate in an engaging way in all written communications. Key to achieving this is the use of the active rather than the passive voice. The active involves statements such as, 'We will send you your bill.' The customer knows who is doing it (we), what is happening, (will send), and to whom it is happening (you). The passive voice, so often used in business, employs phrases such as, 'A bill will be sent.' Most customers naturally get confused and irritated by such statements. You have no sense of who is doing what. The active voice is a much more engaging style of writing. The passive voice is the last refuge of the bureaucrat who does not want to be blamed for anything.

The culture of companies has changed immeasurably over the last twenty years – many companies are barely recognisable. The old attitude of folded arms and 'It won't work here' is passing away. Language itself has played a part in moving people from the old-fashioned ways, as it has become more open and accommodating.

For international communications, it is worth remembering that design is a universal language. A crucially important reason why you should invest in design is that if you use design to communicate there are no cultural barriers or language problems.

Give us a KISS

Have you ever gone to a restaurant and been overwhelmed by the choice? Or looked at a catalogue that goes into so much detail you just get confused and give up? This is stupid. And that is where the KISS principle comes in. As wise hands in business will always tell you, Keep It Simple, Stupid! This is a powerful principle with a great deal to recommend it.

To understand the essence of the KISS principle, see how stupid certain software products are. There is a very popular word-processing package that has so many irritating, redundant and ludicrous buttons that the user can easily spend hours trying to undertake the most simple task. The software is so crass, and difficult to use, that there are tiny robotic personalities that spring up on screen to try to help you use your computer. But, if the software had been designed from the beginning using the KISS principle, the problems would not occur.

An element of mystery

If you run a road haulage company, and you own a fleet of trucks, even one or two, how can you get noticed? You have a medium with which to communicate: the surfaces of your vehicles. But everybody is trying to do that – everybody is trying to shout loudly using design. What alternative could you try? Sometimes one of the most powerful urges we have is to discover, or unravel, a mystery. This is a compulsion that you can use. Consider what it would cost to paint your vehicles completely white, in so far as it is possible. Apart from tyres and windscreens, can you get them snow-white all over? As a part of this brand-building exercise, can you afford to clean them regularly?

This might involve the expense of buying a jet-wash machine, and asking your drivers to clean the vehicle every morning. If you can afford it, why not do it? Now alone this approach will certainly attract attention, and your vehicles will be noticed, because nobody else looks like that. You have already won half the battle. However, to really capitalise on this effect, you want to give people a way to try to explain the mystery. Somewhere prominent, but in quite small type, write your phone number, or, better still just a website URL.

It should not be necessary to write anything at all other than the contact detail. The very white vehicles, kept scrupulously clean, say everything you could want to say about your haulage firm. If you really want to push the boat out, you could also ask your drivers to wear white suits. Think about what this adventure in cleanliness and minimalism would really cost. Over time, it could make a very big impression.

Let there be lights

When I studied at retailing college we were taught that the best way to get prospective customers into your store was to have as little encumbrance to them as possible. In summertime that means you should leave the door open, and, as I mentioned earlier, *never stand in your doorway*. In wintertime, retail theory used to suggest, you would leave the door open and blow warm air into the street to attract freezing passing trade.

Today, of course, that energy consumption is utterly unacceptable. However, in the absence of heat, there is another deeply held desire that humans lust for, and that is light. By making use of coloured film or shades, stained glass or whatever, combined with low-energy light bulbs, you can make a big impression, and draw in passing trade at minimal environmental or economic cost.

More fun with names

There is a vegetarian restaurant in Brighton with the extremely distinctive and memorable name of WAI-KIKA-MOO-KAU, which is presented in capital letters combined with their logo of a smiling cow looking rather sweet. As vegetarians, the proprietors are saying in effect, 'Why kick a moo cow?' Or, more simply put, 'Why be horrible to cows?' The name is strange indeed, resonant and funny.

Inside the restaurant the proprietors clearly use lighting beautifully, and the place feels comfortable but not too smart, so it is not intimidating. Basically, the restaurant is just a lovely place to be, and the brand is surprisingly well known. So why kick a moo cow?

Why intimidate?

Not being intimidating is an important point to remember. One of the reasons why McDonald's outlets look so deliberately childlike is that the company specialise in not intimidating people. Restaurants can be intimidating, sometimes deliberately so. But that is a very tricky end of the market to go for. For mass sales to mass customers, make sure you do not look intimidating.

Creating a mood to match your customers

A favourite haunt of students in Brighton, year after year, decade after decade, is the Dumb Waiter café. It has a well-chosen combination of features and an environment well suited to the desires of young people. The food is simple and cheap. It feels almost like a youth club with dozens of photos, posters and leaflets promoting clubs wall to wall. It also has some very stylish modern paintings.

It looks down at heel, a mess, even, but it is clearly loved both by the clientele and the owners. The great skill has been, over time, to combine successfully the natural instinct younger people have to highlight and collect items that are visually rich within an overall, ordered aesthetic.

Delicacy in typography

Sometimes a great brand is about a tiny detail. It was the great design consultant Neil Svensen who first pointed out to me how a small detail can define everything. There used to be hundreds of bright orange vans circling London belonging to the office supplies company Dudley Limited and bearing the insignia 'Dudley'. With thick white type and a big white chevron as a logo, it looked like a typically non-descript example of rather incompetent corporate design. At the same time, the mobile-phone company Orange had just launched a highly sophisticated visual identity developed by Wolff Olins, based on white type appearing on a very similar orange background, just like Dudley.

However, the two could not have looked more like chalk and cheese. There was no possible comparison between them. Dudley looked awful, Orange looked great. What Neil Svensen pointed out to me was that the only real difference between the two was 'delicacy in typography'. But what a huge difference that is! The great media analyst Marshall McLuhan speaks of 'typography' rather than 'the written word', because he felt that the way words were *presented* was a large part of their meaning. This is true, a phenomenon generally referred to as the 'authority of type'.

Sweet smell of success

How this research was conducted or validated I do not know. However, it is said that smell is the sense most closely linked to memory. It is highly evocative. Retailers, and also shrewd property vendors, have long known the advantages that can accrue through wise use of manufactured smells and scents.

Many large supermarkets have in-store bakeries with the specific objective of pumping the wonderful smell of baking bread into the store to make the shoppers salivate and buy more. It is an old adage, that if you really want to sell your property, it makes sense to bake coffee beans in your oven and allow the smell to drift through the house. This will drive prospective buyers mad with desire to buy, or so they say.

How can you create the right smell for your customers? Is it as simple as putting beautiful flowers in your reception? Should your colleagues be encouraged to wear perfume or cologne? Think about how smell can positively or negatively affect your business.

Public relations

This is a huge topic that needs to be considered carefully by every small business. A good starting point is just to consider what proportion of the stories in your national, regional or local newspaper were put there deliberately by commercial enterprises for commercial purposes. You may be quite shocked to learn that it is 50 per cent or more. Think when you look at each article: which company or person stands to gain from this? And ask how *you* can gain by raising your profile in the press.

The first thing to remember is that the press want stories, and features, and they have a lot of space to fill, regularly. The question is one of how best to fill it. Most newspapers and magazines operate on quite tight budgets, and they are very open to offers of free work. So, if you run a firm of builders and decorators, think how much time you could offer to a newspaper, and then contact the editorial office. It may be that the property section of your local newspaper will do a feature on a dream house, designed by some top local architect or designer. You could start by pitching the idea to local estate agents. You could see if they have an exceptionally interesting property that might benefit from some radical design treatment.

If you can find such a property, contact a local newspaper and say that you are prepared to do up the place, for no charge, to the property editor's specifications, in exchange for a feature and some mention of your firm. This could turn into a range of possible stories along the lines of:

- LIGHTHOUSE CONVERSION MAKES DREAM HOME
- OLD SCHOOLHOUSE BECOMES OASIS OF GREEN
- TOP LOCAL STYLIST CREATES DREAM HOME

Newspapers and magazines are full of these kinds of profiles of interesting properties. Your contribution will be to make it happen, and, in exchange, make sure that any press coverage mentions your firm as 'the expert decorating firm XYZ developed this property'.

It is certainly true that editorial in a newspaper or magazine has much more impact than an advert. Our eyes are normally following the stories and features, and avoiding the adverts wherever possible. When a newspaper or magazine article mentions XYZ as 'expert decorators', that label sticks. You have taken the authority and power of the newspaper and magazine brand, and given it to yourself.

The heart of good PR is building relationships of trust and mutual understanding with journalists and feature writers. It is a good starting point to cultivate relationships with local journalists by writing to them positively if you see articles or pieces they have written with which you agree. The power of the press is legendary, so get it to work for you. There is no great mystery here: you can do your own PR brilliantly, if you can think like a journalist.

 Branding and other techniques . . .

Product association

The essence of branding is to create a complete link between what you do and the product category. Great examples of this are the vacuum cleaner that's known simply as a hoover, and the tampon being similarly synonymous with Tampax. The latter example is particularly interesting. The name Tampax sounds very similar to the word 'tampon'. But users would like to be quite specific about what they want. If you ask for a Tampax you know what you are getting. A tampon is a very general description of a range of possible products.

In the computer industry, there are many examples of companies grabbing a category meaning with their product brands. A Zip Drive, Windows computer, or even IBM-compatible, a statement that refers directly to Intel and Microsoft and has nothing to do with IBM!

Think about how your product name can help people gain a better understanding of what they are actually trying to do. If you get this right, it will help ease speech, and help everyone understand each other better. If what you do is important, but difficult for people to understand, name it, and make that name your brand. If you get it right your customers will do your marketing for you, every time they open their mouths.

Satisfaction guaranteed!

A great friend of mine talks often about GTS, which she says, means 'guaranteed to satisfy'. Perhaps the small but long-lasting hamburger chain Maxwell's represents a good example of GTS. All the things you might want to see on a menu if you like not too challenging food are there. On a bigger scale TFI Friday have done the same thing: burgers, steaks, banana split and milkshakes, as well as some great vegetarian options. It is not about haute cuisine, but rather giving people a reason to visit you. Often, a guarantee of satisfaction is enough.

The GTS principle can apply to any business. If you run a firm of head hunters, you might make a rule that for each serious enquiry you receive you will either send three great applicants, or take the time and trouble to send your client to a competitor who can. What do your clients get out of this? A guarantee of satisfaction. If that isn't a reason to keep coming back, again and again, I don't know what is. This concept can be taken a stage further. If a plumber does a good job and leaves a sticker on the boiler: ANY PROBLEMS CALL 0789 1234567, they may get repeat business forever.

Play a long game

Twelve years ago I went to work for Neil Svensen and his colleagues. We built up a great design business with over a hundred staff. Anyone could see from the start that Neil would go far. But did that stop us going bust? Not at all. Early on, the business, in its first incarnation, had to be wound up, and creditors got most of what they were owed. The creditors' meeting was held in June 1990. A wonderful small print firm called Martin Edwards were owed quite a lot. They attended the meeting and said to Neil, in the depths of a horrible recession, at a liquidators' meeting, 'We are not pointing any fingers, but there is £20,000 of our money in your business.' But they said no more.

Then at Christmas 1990, when we were trying to start again, a case of wine arrived from Martin Edwards printers. Now that was a very big and clever thing to do. We were happy, and we remembered them well. Martin Edwards became a big brand for us. I don't thing they ever sent wine again, but we gave them work. In fact we gave them everything we could. Over the next six years we must have placed over £300,000 of print with them. They looked ahead, understood a situation, they were cool, and it worked.

The FCUK factor

A simple but brilliant device for shouting loud is to use ideas around the incredibly successful French Connection United Kingdom advertising and branding campaigns. We are all very alive to swear words. They have tremendous shock value because society has no idea where to put them. There was a super advert for KLM City Flyer service, who used a small commuter jet made by Fokker for their short haul routes. Their slogan was:

It's all business class on this Fokker

Put the brother on the wall

This is a line from the brilliant Spike Lee film *Do the Right Thing*. It is also an important component of the plot. The film is set in a predominantly black area in one of North America's typically racially segregated cities. The action focuses on a pizza parlour run by a white Italian family serving a largely black clientele. On the walls of the café are pictures of white Italian heroes. So the title is really a question – in fact, a key question is asked by one of the black, regular customers: 'Why don't you have any pictures of black African heroes on the wall?'

In the film, this seemingly trivial point spirals out of all proportion leading to violence and even a small riot. The point? It is the customers who finance the restaurant. It can be not just arrogant but even offensive to pay no regard to customers' tastes and desires.

Do something bizarre, yet unforgettable

It may not make commercial sense – you have to make up your own mind – but it can be very powerful to do something unique. Radio 3, my favourite station, has a small audience, but they tend to be quite cultured. Some of that audience are decision makers in the arts, media and film. A great tragedy of Radio 3 years ago was that it stopped at midnight, an error that used to drive me berserk. One night I was lying half asleep expecting programming to end, when a voice came on to announce that the hour from midnight until 1 a.m. had been produced by Planet 24, the television production company. And then, quite magically, I heard the sound of quite heavy and persistent rain, delivered through my radio for sixty minutes. It is of course a beautiful sound. And I came to remember what Planet 24 had done, and told my friends about it for years afterwards.

Employ people who look different. There is massive evidence to suggest that some measure of systemic racism prevails across almost all businesses. For unknown reasons many white business people feel disinclined to employ nonwhites. This is stupid and a missed opportunity. A huge pool of talent exists waiting to be snapped up if you can make the tiny step to realising that racial discrimination is ridiculous. And, as your business grows with a manifest rejection of racist or homophobic attitudes, you will begin to attract more candidates from these significant minorities. This virtuous circle can help build your brand to improve the calibre of your workplace without increasing costs.

However many things you do, be known for one of them

Working in a design company I have seen many illustrators pass through trying to obtain work. It is often the case that those who develop their work into a particular 'style' can end up winning the most business. This is because designers cannot think what should be done and by whom if the options are not clearly visible. 'So-and-so can do anything, so what will I use them for?' Rather, the designer has to think, 'So-and-so does *that*, and *that* is what I want for this job.' Although specialisation might limit the type of work you do, the mind often works by choosing from what it remembers, rather than imagining what it does not.

That's why you can help potential clients to choose you over others, because what you do is known, and you're known for what you do. It's a question of association. You've heard of being spoiled for choice. If you offer too many choices, you may not get chosen at all.

CHAPTER SIX

Building trust with customers

Chapter outline

Why do people choose your business rather than a bigger chain? How do you seem less intimidating and remote? How can you thrive by showing more people why so many local people trust you? In this chapter we'll be addressing those questions and more.

Increasing customer loyalty

A successful brand signifies trust to customers. Creating this meaning for customers is therefore a significant part of building your brand. Over time, customers come to associate a successful brand with a successful and trusting relationship. This is a long-term investment that will increase customer loyalty, and therefore your profits. What does trust mean in a business relationship? Here are some tips to help you build this trust.

Trusting relationships are harder to attain in an online environment, where you may not ever meet or even speak to your customers. But trust is still a central ingredient of an online brand. In the second half of this chapter I look specifically at the implications of the online environment for building trust with customers.

Trusting relationships

Trust is the feeling of confidence that people have in one another in a successful relationship. It is based on delivering on promises and doing this consistently. When you open a bottle of Coca-Cola you know exactly what is going to be inside. When you go to your favourite restaurant you know that the food and atmosphere will be just to your taste, every time, without fail.

As well as consistency, some other elements that build trust are honesty and openness about what you are doing, and why you are doing it. Your brand is about how your customers feel about your company, and, if they trust you to do a good job and deliver as you promise, then they will feel good about your business. If, from experience, your customers know that you and the business you represent are honest and reliable, then they will start to feel confident in your brand. They will feel confident that they know exactly what they will get when they order goods or services from you. With increasing consumer confidence come the increasing sales that lead to business success.

Trust is reinforced repeatedly by what you do, and confidence is often hard won. It is also easily lost, so, when things are going well, remember that the confidence your customers have is envied by your competitors and is the key to winning, and losing, business. As your business grows you may find your resources stretched. Be honest with your customers about what you can deliver and when. If at some point you have to tell your customer that you don't have the capacity or capability to deliver what they need, you may lose a sale. But you won't lose the customer.

Three elements of trust

So trust is built through the three key elements consistency, responsiveness and honesty. My clients know that they can usually get hold of me on the telephone, and if I am busy I will always call them back within a few hours, even if it is just to let them know that I can't do much right now, but will have done what they need from me by the end of the week.

Gaining the trust of your customers requires treating them well and going out of your way to make sure that they are happy with the goods or services you are supplying them with. It also requires that you can give them honest and clear information about the status of whatever you are doing for them. You may need to train people to help you to provide good customer service. But, if you invest in customer care, you will reap what you sow.

Satisfied customers will not only be returning customers, but they will also do your marketing for you. Word of mouth is the best way to generate new sales. When they trust you, your customers will tell others about your business. If your customers trust you they will also be much more honest about their requirements. You can therefore more easily provide them with what they need, and so they will be still more satisfied with your product or service.

In the early days of the design consultancy Rufus Leonard I used to make it my job to run an analysis of where our business was coming from. Fairly consistently, about 85 per cent each year came from customers we had at the start of the year. This is quite typical. It is infinitely easier to get more business from an existing customer than it is to persuade someone completely new to trust your company. That is what the idea of an account executive is all about. By keeping key customers happy, you win more business.

Maintain adequate communication

Ensure that you are in frequent communication with your customers. This is perhaps the most important single thing you can do to build trust. It means listening to your customers, which is one thing that is often easier for a smaller business than a large corporation to do effectively. You can listen properly and you can make decisions quickly to act upon what you hear.

I had a problem with my mobile-telephone company in 1999, complained and, after some time, was sent an apologetic fax and offered some compensation for the rude treatment received. I accepted their apology and again felt happy with the company. But, when exactly the same problem returned some time later, I understood that they did not actually listen. They had not changed the way they act, only written a hollow apology. They had not changed their processes, so the problem came around again.

By contrast, my local food store changed the brands of coffee they stock. I tried the new brand but it wasn't so good. When I told them they said that other customers had also commented about this. A week later the original brand of coffee was on sale there again.

As a small business you will be able to hear your customers, and make decisions quickly about if and how to respond to their comments. As you grow, be sure to continue to pay attention to what your customers say to you. Big businesses can do this too. In 1996 at a seminar I chaired entitled 'Managing Communications in New Media', Simon Housen-Green, the Internet manager of Sky TV, said, 'Why would I want to commission very expensive research about my TV programmes, when people will discuss them at length, voluntarily in chat rooms? I can simply read what they write, which is better and cheaper.'

Make sure that there is sufficient flexibility in your products and services to respond to your customers' needs. You may need to think through and plan the processes that enable your business to listen carefully to customers and quickly implement changes to what you do. If you don't, then a smaller competitor that can and will listen and may start to take away your customers.

Making it easy for the customer

Another way for smaller businesses to seize advantage and build customer trust is to make it easy for customers to do business with you. Form-filling and lengthy bureaucratic processes are painful for customers and more often than not wholly unnecessary. Insisting, for example, that you have a purchase order in place before commencing work may be a very sensible business process; but if you do not trust your customer then perhaps you shouldn't be doing business with them at all. Especially in a large business, the process of raising a printed purchase order may be painful and time-consuming for a manager who wants to buy your services. That said, purchase orders are compulsory in the best run companies. It is a question of balance.

In the delicate process of acquiring a new client, your competitor who simply goes ahead and delivers the goods with an appointment letter followed by invoice may well tempt them away. A purchase order is a necessary minimum requirement for many businesses and you can understand why. But, if your client is a rock-solid concern like the BBC, who cannot go bust, and if there are numerous letters and emails that confirm your appointment and the price, perhaps you can take a commercial judgement to do without. Once we were commissioned to do a lot of very expensive work by a big company, very quickly. In three weeks the bill reached £23,000. Our client then said he could not sign off more than £10,000 and that was all he would pay.

We stood by our invoices, and eventually most of them were paid. But a senior manager of this long-standing blue chip client said to us afterwards, 'When you find an unfamiliar face from a familiar company, be on your guard.' It is a lesson worth remembering.

You must make these judgements, but think about removing obstacles to business that demonstrate that you do not trust your customers. If you don't trust them, then they sure won't trust you.

Building trust – four key questions (and a few more)

1 **Do you trust your customers, and they you?** How could you demonstrate the confidence you have in them? Show them that you trust them, and if you don't then consider whether you should be doing business with them at all.

2 **Are your communication channels kept open and easy to navigate?** Do you always return calls promptly? Do you and your staff always listen carefully to everything your customers say? Do you send small gifts and cards to your customers at every opportunity? Of course, you must never offer any kind of bribe, but the value of something very small, inexpensive, personal and ideally funny is invaluable. Go out of your way to demonstrate that you are thinking of your customers and that you value their business. Think about how you can make your communications special. Be sincere: hollow communications are ultimately damaging to your customer relationships.

3 **Do you offer the best possible customer service?** If a customer complains, see the problem from their perspective, be open and take responsibility for ensuring that your customer's concerns are dealt with to their satisfaction. Remember, the fallout from one unhappy customer can counteract the good recommendations of many happy ones.

4 **Do you do more than your customers expect?** Be careful not to promise more than you can deliver. Try to deliver early, or add something in for free. What else does your customer need that you can help with? If you can't help them can you recommend another business that could? Be a partner as well as a supplier. Value your customer relationships rather than just sales. The most profitable client relationship my design company ever had was with a major multinational, and it was my job to manage the account. We developed a perfect relationship with the client. We did whatever he asked, and he paid

whatever we invoiced. This process carried on to mutual ease and satisfaction for two years.

Trust in the online world

Whatever your business, you are likely to have some dealings with the Internet. (Chapter 7 looks at the Internet in much more detail.) For smaller businesses the Internet offers a massive opportunity to look bigger, and to reach a global market. But when you don't physically meet with your customers, and with concerns about Internet security being continually reported in the press, how can your business build trust with your customers online?

First, take a look at some famous recent Internet successes and failures. During the middle and late 1990s some entrepreneurs and investors discovered the Internet. They found a unique opportunity to sell goods to massive, global markets without having to support chains of stores and carry unnecessary stock. Web-based shopping will change the way we buy many consumer goods, but only if customers have confidence in the brands they find online. They must be confident that, when they type in their credit card details, they will be kept secure and they will be charged the correct amount. They must be confident that the right goods will arrive.

The famous failure of Boo.com can be directly attributed to that company's ill-fated attempt to build trust with its potential customers. Boo.com spent unfeasible amounts of cash on advertising in the hope that this would establish their brand as trustworthy. How is it that the online bookstore, Amazon.com has managed to attract and retain enough customers to survive when Boo.com did not? The answer is that it is mostly to do with appropriate use of Internet technology. Boo.com failed to impress potential customers with sophisticated graphics and clever animated screens: very few customers experienced the Boo.com website in the way that was intended. Amazon, on the other hand, has never tried sophisticated graphics but actually engages its computers in a task that they can do well: allowing users to search through massive amounts of information about published books and music.

Customers of Amazon can search and browse their massive database of publications with no obligation to buy. One lesson for any business that proposes to trade solely on the Internet is that it must provide tools or information that potential customers can enjoy, even without spending money. Over time, Amazon customers have gained the confidence to place an order. Once an order has been placed, Amazon is meticulous about keeping its customers informed about their orders. Customers receive emails at each stage of their order: when it has been accepted, when it has been processed, when the goods have been dispatched.

The rules for building trust online certainly include communicating well, delivering consistently and offering good customer service. Most importantly it must be easy for customers to do business with you online: your website must work for all potential customers.

There is of course another aspect to branding, and that is fame. Time after time, research into financial services shows people will buy insurance or a pension from a company they have 'heard of'. Part of the genius of Amazon was to gain 'first-mover advantage'. Think about this aspect of brand building with regard to unique selling strategies described in other chapters. Because Amazon was the first bookstore on the Internet, it built a huge reputation through global press coverage. Naturally, no company can do that twice, but in a different area, on a smaller scale, think what you could do? If you are 'Healthy Suffolk', a food company famous for your strong stance against the air transport of food, use press interest in your political position to promote your brand. Remember that Amazon became famous by doing something new, different, modern and relevant. What can you do that fits that description?

What should you consider when using the Internet to help build your brand?

Email and building trust

Email is convenient and fast. If your customers use email it can be a great way to make your communications with them more responsive and less cumbersome. To illustrate some of the pitfalls to watch out for, here is a story about my recent experience when dealing with a small firm of solicitors who were helping me to buy a property.

I was delighted to receive an email from my solicitor. I had not expected this and it created for me an impression that they weren't actually as slow and dull and full of cobwebs as one might otherwise have expected solicitors to be. It seemed that because they used email they were surprisingly modern. This led me to think that they would be likely to do their work more efficiently, quickly and cost-effectively. I felt happy in my choice of firm, read the email and replied.

While it is good that my solicitors use email, I noted a number of things about its use. The following observations are common for the way many small businesses use email, and, while some of these observations may be trivial, their combined effect was to weaken my confidence in their online brand:

■ **Who is the email actually from?** The email I received was from my solicitor but the email address was someone.else@mysolicitors.com. By getting someone else to send and receive his email, my solicitor was, I felt, missing the point somewhat.

■ **Did they get my reply?** My reply was sent within an hour or so of my receiving the email from my solicitor. A week later I decided to call them to make sure that they got it OK. They had, but they did not take the trouble to respond, and that is almost rude. Normally it is safe to assume that people receive email, because if they don't then it will bounce back with an error message within an hour or so. But even so, if you are providing a service it pays to be attentive.

■ **So who were these people anyway?** This firm of solicitors had done work for me before, so I did actually know all that I needed to about them. But out of curiosity I pasted their domain name, 'mysolicitors.com', into my web browser. Not only was there no web page there, but there was a blatant advertisement for the services of their Internet service provider (ISP). So my solicitors merely had a domain name but no web presence.

Think carefully about how the image of your business is projected online. It is best if emails are from the person they say they are from – anything else must surely end in confusion. If you receive an email from a customer, but have nothing to say to them just yet, why not just send a short acknowledgement? This is not uncommon practice in traditional, paper-based correspondence and it is extremely easy and quick to do with email.

Frequently check and reply to email! Frequent email users will expect a reply within hours, so work out a system that enables you to do this. One other note about email: don't spam! Spamming is sending out bulk, unsolicited email. People will try to sell you lists of email addresses. But many people consider unsolicited mail to be an invasion of their privacy. Remember, one bad reaction can be very bad for business, and news travels fast on the Internet.

Your website

A simple website is much better than no website at all. I often go to websites just to get the telephone number or postal address of a business. No great expense would be required to provide a web page with these details and a much more consistent online presence would be created.

Big, established companies can use their websites to reinforce their own well-known brand name and identity. They often spend a lot of money with design agencies. But, if you're a smaller business, people won't necessarily know who you are, so a massive investment in a website may not be justifiable.

Use a simple website as a way to provide background information about your company. You may not gain much new business this way, but, for your existing customers and people you are recommended to, your website is an easy first stop for finding out more about you.

Here are some things to consider when creating your website; each will help to win the trust of customers and potential customers:

- Show that you are **real people** by posting pictures of yourself and members of staff on your site.
- Make your **contact details** obvious. People often go to a company website just to get their telephone number or postal address.
- If you want to **sell directly** from your website, offer ordering through a secure server. Your ISP should be able to offer this.

When your website is built, and you are happy with it, make sure your web address is printed on all your stationery and business cards.

Endorsements

People need to believe in you, but why should they? The answer is, there can be no more ringing endorsement than that given by customers. When trying to approach anybody for the first time, whether by letter, email or telephone, often the best way to start is to state who else you work for. When in the design industry in a sales capacity, I would usually say on making contact for the first time, 'Hi, my name's Paul and I am calling from the design company Rufus Leonard. Our clients include BBC, Shell, Lloyds TSB and Mercedes.'

Beyond this, not much more needed to be said. The prospective customer got the following information instantly:

- This firm is credible.
- It has fantastic clients.
- These high-quality companies have chosen this company over all others.
- This firm has passed my supplier-assessment procedure.
- I will not get sacked for employing these people, because their credentials are impeccable.

This last point is the important one. It used to be the proud boast of IBM, the computer industry giant, that nobody ever got sacked for using IBM. It is clearly much harder for a small company to make this kind of boast, but there are other ways to inspire confidence. If you have a good product, you have nothing to be afraid of. I have a friend who is a fashion agent and one of her first comments to a prospective shop buyer is, 'Do you want to call one of my other customers to see how they like the collection?'

Another good system is to collect any letters satisfied customers may have written, and include these in your future proposals as an appendix. There can be no better way to complete a proposal document than to include a positive statement from happy clients.

Writing proposals

This critical aspect of winning business is frequently neglected, although it is the most important for any business based on the awarding of sizable contracts with either companies or consumers. The heart of showing your business to be big enough for the job is the proposal. For a small business, there are quite a few things you can do to beef up proposals.

Most importantly, take an interest in your prospective customer, find out something about them, read their brochure or annual report, look at their website, and introduce what you write with a positive endorsement of what they are about, possibly along these lines:

As the largest health authority in Norfolk, you have responsibility for 730,000 people in an area of 800 square miles. To meet this task, you employ the most stringent project-management systems. Our company is dedicated to fitting in with those systems to provide a complete solution to your requirements.

Provide the key details of your organisation, including:

- who you are
- what you do
- how you do it
- profiles of key people
- customer endorsements

If you are a very small company, and trying to win business in a bigger league than the one in which you usually operate, you can try a technique that can work well. It involves going into a fair amount of detail regarding how you would approach the work.

For example, I recently awarded a £12,000 contract for extensive work on repairing dry rot in my flat. A very large firm submitted a cost proposal that was very professionally bound, with beautiful typography and all the other things that big companies do well. But there was not much in the proposal of relevance to me. However, a much smaller firm wrote out a very detailed explanation of what they were going to do, and listed every single job that comprised the whole, so I could see exactly where my £12,000 was going. So I gave them the job.

In the design industry, this approach has caused great consternation, because it is called 'free pitching', and is disapproved of by many trade associations because it amounts to charitable work that small design companies can ill afford to do.

However, in the advertising industry, which is far more developed than the design industry, clients recognise that this is perhaps the only way sensibly to pitch for work. So new-business sales people from advertising agencies hawk around a general portfolio of work, hoping to get on a 'pitch list'. From this point onwards, the prospective client will usually pay a fee for three agencies to produce some pitch work.

But the dilemma in the design industry, and many others, is that clients can be generally reluctant to pay for the cost of tendering.

However, Shell have paid suppliers to pitch for design contracts, and they certainly get their money's worth, many times over.

As a smaller company wishing to grow, you have to reconcile yourself to these tensions. It is often said that starting a business from scratch is the hardest job in the world. You basically have to work and work and work, for very little money, to build a reputation. Maybe you have to do a first job for cost, or free. As you become established, it gets easier, but do not underestimate the task.

If you haven't pitched for business from a large organisation before, you will have to be prepared for the fact that the tendering procedure of many of them is antiquated in the extreme. It was my misfortune to be huddled, with about a hundred other design companies, in a Ministry of Defence tower block in West London, in the depths of the 1990 recession, pitching for a contract to provide design services.

The ministry had circulated a huge questionnaire and now invited the competing companies to ask questions. The situation was bizarre, because the questionnaire asked amazingly detailed questions, such as the cost we would charge for photographic linen in Years 1, 2 and 3 of the contract. My colleagues and I, with many years' experience of the industry, did not know what photographic linen was.

The key skill is to be able to show that your company is not stale, rather it is new, vibrant, growing, representing the future, not the past. You can do that by:

- being different
- being entertaining
- being personal
- being accessible
- showing that you care
- communicating passion
- making them feel as if they are sharing in the adventure of your company
- giving a guarantee of personal service and attention

It is never a good idea to knock the competition, but, if you present your business in the right light, your prospective customer will do it all for you.

An appropriate approach to sales

The German national economy is in many regards the leader in Europe. The genius of German business is to appreciate one simple, astounding principle or fact about economic life that is so often ignored. That fact is simply that, at the end of each year, there is another year.

The decline in British manufacturing industry can largely be blamed on an insufficient regard for this cardinal principle. So how does an attitude that thinks long-term manifest itself in action? The first rule is to help your customers to buy what they need, and not the maximum you can sell them. Even the most cursory analysis will demonstrate that a customer you keep for a few years is worth many times the value of a big order.

As a responsible, long-term and profit-orientated supplier, you have to make it your job to ensure customers do not buy too much. Think about it. An excess of anything takes up space, gets soiled and puts people off. Don't become responsible for overselling whatever it is you do.

CHAPTER SEVEN

Using the Internet

Chapter outline

The Internet is a wonderful channel for smaller businesses to build bigger brands and gain more customers. In cyberspace, no one can see that your company is small, and that is a huge advantage. This chapter will examine approaches to website development with a focus on matching the appropriate effort to expected results.

IT is *it*!

Despite the notorious dotcom failures, the Internet is not going to go away. Have a look and see how many of your competitors are using it, and how. Websites are great for reaching widely dispersed geographical audiences. Anyone in the world can have access to the most simple of websites. Email is transforming the way many businesses work, with opportunities for people to work in different ways that better suit their chosen way of life.

As your business changes to allow more and more remote working, a level of infrastructure change may be required. Investment in the right infrastructure can save you money and increase productivity further down the line.

Take teleworking, for instance. As well as changes in the culture of a business that may be required in order to profit from increased teleworking, a certain infrastructure is also required. This will enable workers to connect to your company network to view and transfer files that they have been working on. Also, you may want to use a secure email service so that your company email is encrypted as it travels through the Internet.

There are two established approaches to providing an infrastructure for remote access, RAS (Remote Access Service) and VPN (Virtual Private Network). RAS provides users with direct modem access to a server that is located at the business premises and connected into the company network. The user dials directly into the RAS server, and a 'point-to-point' connection is established. The RAS server can be configured to call the user back as part of the connection sequence, so that the company rather than the remote user is billed for the phone calls incurred. For a small number of users, RAS is great because it is easy and cheap to implement.

But, as more people start to use the infrastructure, there are some problems to look out for. With RAS, each connected user requires a modem connected to a phone line. The cost of these dedicated modems and phone lines can mount up, even before you have counted the call charges to remote users who may be far away. An alternative infrastructure, and one that many businesses are currently turning to, enables a 'virtual' VPN. A VPN device is installed at the business premises and connected into the main Internet connection (usually a leased line to a local ISP). The VPN unit is configured to allow the creation of a completely private and fully encrypted 'tunnel' to any other point on the Internet where a remote user is connected.

A VPN tunnel is used by any remote user requiring access to the company network, and provides the same level of security as with the RAS server. The advantage is that many users (thousands) can be supported with one VPN unit, and all users dial into their local ISP, thus eliminating long-distance call charges. Users simply require a 'VPN client' program on their PC and they can access the company network from any Internet connection. To see examples of the VPN architecture, visit www.asitatechnolegies.com.

Your Internet connection

In the office you will probably need a permanent connection to the Internet if your company uses it to any great degree. With the advent of DSL, or 'Digital Subscriber Line', this is now much more affordable than it once was. Your ISP should be able to provide you with a quite fast, permanent connection for a fixed price. The great thing about DSL is that you don't need any new wires installed: the service can be delivered using any normal telephone line; and, what's more, you can continue to use the telephone line for voice calls as before. There is more than one kind of DSL service including Asynchronous (ADSL), Synchronous (SDSL) and others. Sometimes these are collectively referred to as 'xDSL'.

Once you do have a permanent Internet connection, your company and staff will have access to the most versatile communications and information resource there is. But with a permanent connection you will need to think about security: a permanent connection is more open to Internet hackers than a dial-up. So you will need a firewall device to protect your company network. A firewall device prevents certain kinds of data passing through your network and makes it much harder for hackers to gain unauthorised access to your data. Finally, you may well want to be able to prioritise certain types of traffic (such as for Internet-based telephone traffic, videoconferencing and other 'real-time' applications) or certain computers on your network. This service, known as 'policy routing', will enable you to make the best use of the bandwidth you have available and can save you having to upgrade the connection as demand grows.

Emerging Internet channels

The Internet has revolutionised many businesses. You have probably used 'the Internet' in one form or another, probably by surfing the World Wide Web on a personal computer or by sending and receiving email. The Internet itself is capable of much more than this, appearing in other devices, and enabling lots of different transactions to take place. For businesses who are moving into the online world, the things that you are most likely to be looking at are the Web and email, but some ideas about what is coming up next and how this fits with these existing services will help you with your business strategy.

In 2000 there was a lot of hype about WAP – Wireless Application Protocol. WAP is the equivalent for mobile devices of HTTP – Hypertext Transfer Protocol – for computers. These are just technologies that enable the transfer of information over the Internet. WAP-enabled mobile telephones are now quite common, but have not yet been used for anything very useful. This is mostly because, as with a personal computer, you currently have to establish a dial-up connection with an ISP in order to receive information. WAP then enables you to receive information in a similar format to web pages. But mobile telephone calls are prone to disconnection, and the WAP infrastructure is still (at the time of writing, at any rate) somewhat flaky. The next generation of mobile telephones is worth watching, however, for it will no longer be necessary to make a dial-up connection. With so-called '2.5G' phones, utilising General Packet Radio Service (GPRS), the data connection will be continuous. Such 'always on' connections should open up the possibility for many more innovative mobile Internet services. GPRS has been widely trailed throughout the UK with corporate users in 2000. At the CeBIT show in Hanover in March 2000 GPRS was the star, and the phones will be widely available by the end of 2001.

More significant today, however, are text messages. Once known only by the obscure abbreviation 'SMS' (for 'Short Messaging Service'), they were named 'text messages' by some very smart person somewhere. Millions are sent each day, many by children. Text messages in the UK are extremely popular, and, with mobile-telephone penetration nearing 100 per cent, this system is definitely of the mass media. Text messages can be sent and received by any mobile-telephone user, but can also be generated through other Internet-connected devices such as personal computers, see www.flytxt.com. Information-based text messages may present opportunities for website owners, and can also produce revenues, because users are often charged for receiving as well as sending them. Some information services do not require any familiarity with computing, because they can be set up simply by sending a text message to a given number, or signing up through an interactive television service.

One brilliant service uses SMS to promote events in Brighton's lively clubs, venues and theatres. By sending a single message to a special number, a user can register their interest in a category of events: music, comedy, theatre etc. Once the user is registered, the service, called Tickets Tonight, will send you a text message on the day of a show when there are seats left and they have been reduced. The text message contains a voucher number that is used to get the discounted ticket.

This service is a good example of the kind of innovative services that are being devised by small businesses in collaboration with business communities such as clubs and other venues. In particular, this SMS technology benefits from the user's being able to sign up straightaway, on the spot, using their mobile to send an SMS. For small businesses, this kind of instant connection is a terrific boon.

As well as on mobiles, the Internet is starting to appear on people's television screens. There are two types of this sort of Internet, with two names: interactive television and TV Internet. Generally, interactive television offers fundamentally restricted access to the Internet, and for good reason. There is no form of filtering that is 100 per cent effective – only by specifying exact web addresses that are authorised can pornography or unsavoury material be avoided. Access to the Internet, with its millions of completely diverse and potentially offensive content is called TV Internet.

Viewing normal web pages on the television is not a very satisfying experience: they have to be remade to work properly on a television screen. Television screens use lower resolution than computer monitors, and, anyway, most people are sitting further away from the television than they would from their computers. In the UK, interactive television comes in a number of flavours: digital cable (from Telewest or NTL), digital satellite (Open ... from Sky), digital terrestrial (from ONdigital), and games consoles (such as the Sony PlayStation).

You may well be able to offer your services through interactive television, especially if you have already started using the Web to deliver information to your customers. Interactive television could enable you to reach a bigger number of people, as more people will probably eventually have access to Internet services through the television than they will through personal computers. To publish time-relevant data on NTL interactive TV, investigate www.diarymanager.com.

In the future many common devices will be connected to the Internet, enabling them to provide more automated and useful services. A common example is the fridge connected to the Internet to allow food to be reordered directly from the shops. Another is cars connected to the Internet so that mechanics can run diagnostics remotely if there is a fault with the engine. Many more examples, some more realistic than others, will come and go over the next few years, but one thing is certain: some of these ideas will be developed into very successful business services, and your business may just be able to profit from the opportunities presented by emerging Internet channels.

Changing the way we work

For a smaller business there is great advantage to be had from the new work paradigm: outsourcing some of the functions of the business (mainly support functions) to another company – one that makes them its core business. This has the effect of reducing the overheads from support staff and office space.

Practical case study in remote working

Do you really need an office? One small business I know operates in an almost entirely 'virtual' way. The core staff all work from home, or from desk spaces that are close to where they live. Everyone uses the Internet a lot for email, and internal meetings are more often than not conducted using the telephone. Audio conferencing enables teams of people located in different places to convene quickly and discuss issues without the need to take hours, or even days, out to travel and meet people. Also, with everyone sitting at their desk or wherever they happen to be, the overhead of the meeting room can be eliminated.

Diarymanager.com manages itself in this way. The managing director works at home in Brighton; the development team are based in central London and Cambridge; and the sales team are usually on the road. The main servers are located in Brighton, but the developers are able to work on these computers from wherever they happen to be, using the Internet. The sales staff have access to a file server where all sales materials can easily be downloaded, wherever they happen to be. A meeting of the key staff typically involves an hour-long audio conference with people in London, Cambridge, Brighton and Dublin joining from their desks or mobile telephones. With no meeting room to pay for, no travel expenses or time spent travelling, such a meeting is very productive and convenient for everyone.

You may wonder how diarymanager.com manages to appear businesslike in front of its customers and partners. If you call up the company your call will be taken by a receptionist, who will transfer you to the right person. The diarymanager.com receptionist is there 24 hours a day and is very cost-effective. This is because the infrastructure and staffing of diarymanager.com are rented as a service from Vodafone: for diarymanager.com, this means that one simple, and modest, monthly bill covers receptionists to cover the phones all the time, a place for them to work, the capital costs of their phone system and the management and training of the staff.

Similarly, there is always a need for the sales staff to meet with customers at the diarymanager.com office. So the business has made arrangements to have the use of well-appointed meeting rooms, but not to own the lease or have to pay the electricity and heating bills. The facilities are available as they are required. The business has made the decision to leave property management to property-management businesses, and telephone answering to telephone-answering businesses.

Many small businesses also outsource their accounting function, often to a firm of accountants who maintain all the books, make payments, chase invoices, manage the payroll and so on. Once these kinds of services are established they allow you to focus on your business proposition, keeping things simple and therefore less stressful. Outsourced services can also be turned on and off easily: if diarymanager.com were to receive no calls one month, they would just pay a small retainer fee. When the phone gets busy they pay the cost of dealing with those calls. But since ringing phones usually means that business is good then this all stacks up for that business.

There are other issues to consider with this virtual model of working: most obvious is the question of how teams can really get to know each other, work well together, without bonding on a daily basis. It would be reasonable to expect a virtual company to spend a fair proportion of the money it saves on renting an office space on team-building exercises: trips to conferences and symposia, or just days out in the countryside. Much office time in traditional companies is spent chatting, gossiping and socialising. There is nothing wrong with this, but it does mean that less work is done. An alternative, then, would be for employees to work more productively but for less time each week. Then, with a day or more each week to spare, and with the overheads saved through this, the company could pay for a day out somewhere for the staff!

The day out should be optional: many people may fill their new free time with activities with people in their local community, or they may be able to see their family or look after children. These are the things that we often can't find the time for if we are commuting daily to an office, and that prevents some otherwise very good workers in your business from working with you. And, of course, this is all a much more environmentally sustainable way to manage business, actively reducing the amount of harmful emissions that are a direct result of unnecessary travel.

It is not just office-orientated kinds of business that can benefit from reviewing how things could be done. Consider how your business can fit with this new way of working. Perhaps you should be delivering goods to people at home rather than expecting them to come in the car on their way to or from work? Maybe you too can benefit from, or even provide, the kinds of virtual services that I have been describing.

The move towards living and consuming services and goods more locally, whether in business or personal life, is an essential change that will impact, in a good way, on all parts of the community. Businesses and the entrepreneurs who create and run businesses are the most proactive agents of change in society today, so consider how you can help to change the way we work.

Websites

The global reach of the Internet makes it possible to scale up a web-based operation at phenomenal speed. A single company, Charles Schwab, have been able to dominate the buying and selling of shares across the whole of America in just a couple of years. They need only one location for a few computers, and, once their site is in place, each additional user of their website has marginal impact on the cost of their operations. If a firm wanted to compete on such a scale using manual processing, they would have to hire large numbers of employees, provide them with premises, train them and incentivise them.

Think of it: large computers performing billions of calculations per second and never needing to halt, no coffee breaks, no families, no trips to the loo. In the old economy, the only way to compete was to try to squeeze ever greater marginal efficiency out of employees. This was always hard and often fruitless work that honoured neither party well. The Internet enables businesses to replace boring repetitive jobs that people do badly with machines. The Internet is a new architecture for business with limitless potential. There is little choice but to get involved. And a wonderful opportunity.

Your 'website' is perhaps something of a misnomer. In practice it is more appropriate to think of your 'web process'. If you intend to use your website as a serious business tool, and you should consider this, it should not and cannot be just a brochure. The most effective websites are part of a full Internet strategy that can transform the whole of the way your business works. As such, your website should not be treated as an isolated add-on to your business, and its development should be driven from the top. The process for developing a basic website is actually quite simple. The real art is in adding functionality that will help build your relationship with your customers. So, once you have existing and potential customers visiting your website, you need somehow to keep them coming back. However you choose to do this, it will likely have an impact on most if not all of your existing business processes.

Great website development starts with a clear sense of what you want to achieve. From this point you can move on to very careful review of content and structure. In collaboration with your developer, consider the structure of the site, the homepage and next level of navigation. Consider the user's journey around the site. It can be tempting to structure a website so it imitates or replicates the structure of your business, but is that sensible? What does the user need to know, and how are they going to find that information? A consistent navigational system is a very good idea. Buttons should stay as consistent as possible from page to page. Make sure that you always have a link back to the homepage on every page, perhaps through a text link or link from your company logo.

The golden rule is to remember that computers can do things. They can do wonderful and incredible things. Simply moving your company brochures to the Web is to miss the point. Make sure your site can actually do things for users. One easy way to add meaningful functionality to your site is to use ready-made web applications. These are provided by application service providers (ASPs), who will often provide their application under your company brand in exchange for a fee. This can be much cheaper and quicker than paying to have your own applications developed. Have a look at what applications are out there that you can offer to your users under your own brand: diarymanager.com is one good example and there are many more.

Here are some key questions to ask yourself when you're evolving a web project:

- What do you want your website to achieve?
- Who is this website aimed at?
- What are the key questions or divisions that lead to a content structure?
- What resources will be required each year to manage your website?
- How will you promote your website?
- Who will develop your website and who will host it?

Technology is a challenging medium for project managers. It can be the person who says 'no' who saves the day. If you want the website to be delivered on time and to budget, define what you want at the start and then do not be distracted by any bright ideas that come up during development. You can always include them in the next revision of the website.

People tend not to tell their surgeons where to make incisions, or suggest to chefs how to cook. But everyone has a designer in them bursting to get out. Resist trying to tell the website designer how to do their job, the colours you like and so on. Choose the right development partner and then let them do what you are paying them for.

Website maintenance

A website is for life, not just for Christmas! Developing a website is much more about introducing a new business process than a simple communications project that has a definite end point. As with launching a new logo, a website is just the beginning. On the day it goes live the work starts.

You must have a plan for updating your website: small things change all the time and all your hard work and money will end up having a negative impact on your brand if the information on your site is out of date or simply wrong.

Domain names

If you have not yet registered your business name as an Internet 'domain name', do so immediately. Your domain name is the address for all your Internet communications, email and websites. Any Internet service provider will be able to do this for you. Or go direct to a company such as www.netnames.co.uk. The words you use to describe and promote your business are a very important part of your brand. In the online world words become even more important, so choose them carefully.

Your domain name is an important part of your Internet strategy. In many cases it is a central part of your business identity. The word you choose is used every time someone sends and email to you@yourcompanyname.com and every time someone visits www.yourcompanyname.com. If you have more than one department, or websites aimed at different types of customers, such as partners or resellers, consider how you will incorporate these into your Internet naming. As with any other business communication, consistency is critical.

A new way to work

The Internet is not just about your website. It will certainly include email and this will have an impact on the way you do business. New Internet technologies such as mobile Internet and TV Internet may also come to be an important part of how both you and your customers use the Internet.

The new century has begun with a new feeling about work, with a great deal of change being brought about by technology. The businessman's lounge suit has begun to disappear from view. Serious people in the new media industries rarely wear them, and this is deliberately to demarcate themselves from the old economy, its conventions and restrictions. Not wearing a suit, some people would argue, also shows confidence. You dare to be different. This is not a computing industry preserve. Industrialists such as General Electric's Jack Welch are famous for advocating an informal style of dress.

This increasing informality and easiness is not accompanied by a slowdown in the business drive for increased efficiency, however. Working from home, working on the move, the cellphone and Internet cafés are techniques and tools that allow us to do more work at our own pace, in our own time. For people looking after children these can be useful developments.

As we look ahead at these fantastic machines, a billion networked computers, humming away through the Internet, what are they achieving? Perhaps their greatest gift is to free us from the excessive drudgery of life. They can do the filing, search the records, process the orders and count the money. The basics, especially the dull functions of offices, are being quite quickly liquidated. Accompanying this inevitable trend is a new freedom and opportunity. The birth of the knowledge worker is a very exciting trend. People can spend more time thinking and being creative, and less time managing mundane activity.

These are big changes for everyone. One guiding principle is that it is not about technologies: rather it's the deals that get cut to exploit them. Real experts say they are unsure about the future. Nobody knows how technology will change business and society, but everyone knows it will. There is no time to teach, and nowhere else to learn. So jump in!

Reviewing emerging channels

So, to decide what kind of media to use you need to answer the following questions:

- How much do you currently spend on advertising and other communications by product, and for the whole organisation?
- Is it enough? Too high or too low?
- Who has an overall view on expenditure?
- What do you currently spend on Internet communications?
- How do you evaluate the cost-effectiveness of your communications generally?
- Who are your principal audiences?
- How do you prioritise them?
- What communications do your key audiences attend to?
- How many use the Web at home or work?
- How many have mobiles, and, of them, how many have WAP phones?
- How many may use interactive TV, today and tomorrow?
- How important is your local versus national versus global audience?

Out of this exercise you should begin to develop a feeling for the kind of communications environment in which you operate. Before looking at the character of different communications, it is worth considering in detail one fundamental ground rule. The Internet generally, websites, WAP sites and interactive television are absolutely not primarily advertising media. If you have someone's email address you can send them unsolicited email. If you have their phone number, you can send them unsolicited text messages, but it is generally inadvisable.

What the different channels are for

Websites
An essential medium for posting core information about your company. Instant, global and accessed via a keyboard and mouse, also utilising hypertext and the full power of sophisticated server systems. On your website you can easily:

- sell things
- buy things
- offer any amount of information
- take credit card payments or orders
- recruit staff
- offer search facilities to your databases

And just about anything else you can imagine. The PC-based website is the most flexible communications tool ever invented.

Internet on TV
As we've seen, this is in many ways similar to the above except that it's often accessed without a keyboard, without horizontal scrolling and with no opportunity to print out. It can be used by a computer-illiterate audience, and viewed at an awkward couple of metres rather than 30 centimetres or so. Other pitfalls with interactive TV include relatively low penetration and use (as at December 2000), low screen resolution (lines rather than pixels) and limited set-top-box processing power, caused by the use of a smaller number of cheaper microchips than in a standard PC. This last point seriously limits the degree to which the significant potential functionality of the Web can be used.

WAP services on mobile phones
These offer some of the functionality of the Web, including browsing from page to page and using hypertext links. Unfortunately, the phone keypad will be significantly worse than an interactive TV remote control; the display screen is extremely small; and you have

only one colour and very low resolution. WAP pages have to be written in WML (or wireless mark-up language), and this is both a compression system for data, and a format for presenting it.

Finally, and perhaps most significantly, as we saw earlier, WAP sites require a point-to-point mobile phone call to be established and maintained during interaction. This is exactly as time-consuming and expensive as a voice telephone call. WAP has not proved popular.

Text messages on mobile phones

These are functionally very limited at a maximum of 160 characters per message. The technology is, however, robust, proven and not too expensive. A rate of around 10 pence per SMS sent should be the maximum one pays, and if you are offering a premium service your customers can be charged up to £1 for each SMS they agree to pay for, added to their phone bill. The balance, up to 90 pence per SMS, can be claimed by your business if you provide a service people are prepared to subscribe to. Does £1 seem like a lot to pay for an SMS? Perhaps not if your child is offered a reverse-charge phone-call service to contact you in time of danger.

New Internet business models

Without doubt, the most significant trend on the Internet for consumers in 2000 to 2001 has been www.napster.com. Napster is a P2P (or peer-to-peer) application, whereby some 50 million people have registered to download and swap music files in the popular MP3 format.

What Napster illustrates is that people can share things, and there are giant businesses to be built around sharing. Napster has received a $100 million investment from the global media titan, Bertelsmann. Interestingly, Bertelsmann are simultaneously suing Napster for copyright infringement. At time of writing, it seems Napster will probably be heavily restricted.

Think what Napster proves. It shows that the underlying business model of the Internet is to do things for free, and share things for free. If you accept that people will be passing a wide variety of content around for no charge, how can you make a business that benefits from this?

One way is by analysing how people consume content and then trying to predict what they will want next. Large companies have been analysing data in this way for a long time. This is called 'data mining'. Small companies can do this, too, and it is a great way to learn the important new skill of customer profiling.

The starting point should be to study data-protection legislation, and try to ascertain what you are actually allowed to do (see www.pro.gov.uk/recordsmanagement/dp). It may unfortunately be illegal to look at certain types of data, or you may need to gain your customer's permission in advance. But, having gathered that it is possible to analyse profiles, you then need to consider what is the objective of the exercise.

It should ideally be to ensure customers do more business with you. And, to ascertain how to do that, consider what they want. What drives them?

Deconstructing your business

With the Internet you can take your business apart – literally. And that has tremendous implications for employee benefits, premises costs and general wellbeing. It is certainly true to say that offices are prisons, and the only way to overwhelm our fantastically sophisticated transport system is for everybody to travel at exactly the same time, which is what we do. The result is the rush hour, when people collaborate to make each other uncomfortable.

So how can you build your brand by changing the way you work? Think about what makes a company successful:

- attentive employees
- happy employees
- people who care about the business
- employees who are available 24/7 to serve customers better

Think now about what you would have to do to get your employees to behave in the ways described above. The answer? Give them some freedom. Let them work where they want, how they want. The whole invention of a nine-to-five, five-days-per-week existence was based on the demands of machines, in factories, in cities.

Now everything has changed. We can keep our work, if we are

knowledge workers, on the Internet. This huge trend is generally described as 'server-side migration', and it represents the most fundamental shift in computing that has ever occurred.

If, like me, you use a Yahoo! email account, and pay to have a large, 20MB mailbox, then you have already started the process. Your computer becomes *any* PC, with an Internet browser. You suddenly become free of the constrictions of the office. This is a great liberation.

You can work from home, on the move, travel abroad, and still do your job. Perhaps we are moving towards a situation where the old adage of Confucius is finally coming true: 'When you get the job you want, you never work another day in your life.'

Think about how best your organisation could free itself from the tyranny of office life. How can you offer your current and prospective employees a new deal that gives them the freedom to make more of their lives? If you make the people you work with happy, they will make you happy, as sure as eggs are eggs.

The advantages of server-side computing are almost too numerous to mention, and they can make a major increase to your business efficiency. Examples of server-side systems that you can deploy today include:

- **Email**. Keeping your email on a good web server such as Yahoo! can make life simple and efficient. Any files you want to keep, you can email to yourself. And, using search systems integrated with web services, you can find files quickly and easier.

- **Diary services**. Few people appreciate how significant the movement to server-side computing will be in the critical area of time management. If you want to build your brand, and you are a plumber, think about how convenient it is to let any of your customers book you in, 24 hours a day, seven days a week, over the Internet. The same applies to dentists, doctors, hairdressers, solicitors or anyone else who works on an appointment basis. To make use of free web diaries go to the leading European company in the field, www.diarymanager.com

- **Advanced telephony systems**. One of the main drivers of the communications revolution has been the mobile telephone. You can have any central switchboard, anywhere, transfer callers to a mobile telephone. And that device provides the final component in releasing your employees. The stupid companies have fixed offices, and transfer people perpetually to voicemail. But the

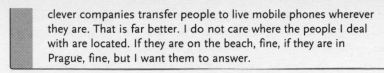

clever companies transfer people to live mobile phones wherever they are. That is far better. I do not care where the people I deal with are located. If they are on the beach, fine, if they are in Prague, fine, but I want them to answer.

The attentiveness that should be the hallmark of every progressive business can be better achieved through a devolved company with diverse locations, delivering happy and attentive staff.

CHAPTER EIGHT

Partnerships

Chapter outline

Big companies and brands are just begging to learn what small companies have always done naturally, namely partnerships. In this chapter I review the reasons for partnering and describe how four small businesses have created successful partnerships that have helped them grow and win new business.

One and one make . . .

The Thai food in your local pub is a great example of new ways to combine old businesses. Small companies can achieve big things by using their distinctiveness to make introductions into much larger concerns.

If you say the word 'partnership' in front of a corporate lawyer, their most common response will be 'no way'. Partnership has a legal meaning that is too often elevated so far as to stop partnerships from happening. Yet partnerships are critical to modern business, especially but not exclusively for smaller businesses and businesses working with the Internet and new media.

One strategy is to find some big friends or, ideally, customers. By associating your business with a well-known brand that has similar values to your own, you can open doors. Another is to team up with like-minded companies to produce something no single company could have done alone.

Managing partnerships can be very time-consuming, but if you choose the right partners you can derive massive benefits for your business. There are many different sorts of partner:

- suppliers and advisers
- complementary businesses
- customers
- other businesses that work with the same customers or suppliers
- government and government agencies

When discussing a partnership relationship with another company it will often be an add-on to some existing or proposed trading relationship. If you build that relationship into a partner, both businesses will benefit from a longer-term, closer relationship than you might otherwise have.

Try listing the benefits of a proposed partnership: you need to understand the benefits to your partner as clearly as you understand the benefits to your business. The benefits in a successful partnership will be equally valuable for each party. In the following case studies I have identified some of the benefits that came to the businesses and their partners.

Case study 1: Rufus Leonard

Rufus Leonard is a leading corporate-identity consultancy based in London. In ten years it has grown from a small, brand-led design company into a successful, brand-led e-business consultancy. Rufus Leonard's clients currently include Aegis, Barclays, BT, Daimler Chrysler, Lloyds TSB, the Post Office, Shell Chemicals, Scandia, Swiss Life and Thus. The company's impressive past and present client list is largely due to its open, partnership-based relationship with each client.

One of the defining moments in the company's growth was the move from designing for print to designing for electronic media. One of Rufus Leonard's longest-established clients, Shell, wanted to start providing documentation and design tools on CD-ROM. The lists of benefits for each partner would have looked something like this:

Benefits to Shell

- manuals and other documents provided on CD-ROM
- huge reduction in the costs of printing and distributing manuals
- creation of a partner with an ongoing capability for producing materials in electronic media
- continuing to work with an established supplier and project team for new media as well as print
- no need to create in-house capability for CD-ROM development

Benefits to Rufus Leonard

- opportunity to expand production capabilities to include CD-ROM
- security derived from a good working relationship with a large corporation
- new resource that could be offered to other clients
- significant addition to the creative portfolio

The relationship between the large corporation and the small design company was mutually beneficial and offered benefits to both concerns that extended far beyond the contacted deliverables of CD-ROM materials on CD-ROM.

Rufus Leonard is still a supplier to Shell, and has successfully developed a long-term relationship with the petrochemicals giant that has been a key to the company's growth and success. Importantly, when pitching for new business, Rufus Leonard was able to talk about its experience with Shell and how it had deployed a new development resource.

It is interesting to see how the true spirit of partnership developed in this relationship. Because electronic media were very new to the design industry in 1993, Rufus Leonard partnered with a 'multimedia' company, who managed the programming side of the project. By early 1994 both Shell and Rufus Leonard could see that this relationship was going to fail to deliver the level of quality that the project required. In a spirit of partnership, the client at Shell said to Neil Svensen, the MD of Rufus Leonard, 'We have to solve the problem – give me some options.'

Svensen got on the telephone for two days and produced a range of proposals for Shell, including finding other suppliers or passing the whole job over to others. But included also was the option of building a programming resource inside Rufus Leonard. This would probably cost Shell a bit more money, but it would guarantee the quality of the product. In the spirit of partnership, Rufus Leonard also committed to bearing as much of the cost as it could.

Together with Rufus Leonard's creative ability, the success of this partnership arrangement provided breakthrough quality to Shell's electronic communications.

Case Study 2: Brighton Media Centre

The Brighton Media Centre (BMC) has grown since 1996 from a small enterprise to become a pioneering umbrella organisation that provides a supportive and flexible structure to both start-up and established media businesses. BMC has grown from one to four buildings and is today the home of around fifty media companies working in a range of disciplines.

BMC is a company built on commitment to partnership. Part of its role now is to nurture partnerships between the small businesses located in BMC buildings. But the defining moment in the growth of BMC was a partnership with government. This is one of the hardest things to do. Small businesses are very different from large organisations.

Like large commercial companies, local and national government are only just learning how to create effective partnerships with smaller businesses. BMC received a Best Practice Award from the Department of the Environment 1997, but the real achievement was the thriving business that BMC has become today.

BMC partnered with Brighton & Hove Council to open their first building bringing benefits to all involved:

Benefits to Brighton & Hove Council

- creation of employment and economic regeneration in central Brighton
- learning about working in partnership with small, emerging, new-economy businesses
- meeting central government regeneration targets
- providing increased access to new-media education and training

Benefits to BMC

- public funding that helped to attract private investment
- increased profile in the city
- experience of working with a large and bureaucratic organisation
- introductions to other potential partners for future developments

At the heart of the BMC concept is a commitment to use partnerships to make life easy for start-up businesses in Brighton. BMC tends to rent out small spaces, with Internet access, sometimes for short terms. The management is very relaxed and informal. Trust develops and small businesses that have grown out of the BMC stay fiercely loyal to it. The founder of the BMC, Ian Elwick, is a hardworking and gentle man. He inspires in people a belief that life is easy and logical. He makes hundreds of deals each day by being light on paperwork, and good on partnership. He has built an empire but has decided not to bleed it dry. He is not a millionaire and does not particularly want to be. He embodies the true spirit of partnership, namely mutual interest. Notice the key word, mutual.

Case Study 3: Asita Technologies

Asita Technologies was formed in 1997 by a group of engineers from Ireland, Germany, Switzerland, France and the UK. They are network technology experts and have produced extensive technology research and development for the European Commission as well as for Cannon Research and the French network infrastructure provider, CS Telecom.

A true 'new economy' company, they cover a massive geographical area and have learned to use new communications technologies very effectively in their work. Most communications between staff are by email and conference calls. They have used their experience of distributed working and organisation to enable them to build partnerships with complementary-technology companies all over the world. With rapid growth they recently opened new offices in the United States in order to focus on selling their advanced network security products.

On one network security project, Asita Technologies worked closely with five other European technology companies: Digital Copyright Technologies Ag, Pijnenburg Custom Chips BV, R3

Security Engineering, Data Communications Technologies Hellas and CS Compagnie des Signaux (France). By partnering, each company could focus on its own area of expertise but jointly deliver a major technological innovation, the world's fastest security encryption chip. Each of these companies derived some or all of the following benefits from the project partnership:

- access to valuable technical expertise
- development of a culture of dealing with international partner companies
- learning to communicate effectively at a distance using new-media technologies
- increased visibility in the marketplace through representing one another locally
- access to a research-and-development contract that they could not have won individually

There has been a lot of talk about the so-called 'new economy'. Although dotcom companies quickly became more famous for their failure than success, an interesting structural change has been taking place in capitalism that is fuelled by technology and is genuinely new. In essence the issue is that bigger companies have become far more vulnerable to more incentivised and fast-footed competitors. The example of Asita Technologies shows how the real talent of the twenty-first century is the few key individuals who can really make a project happen. These people know they own the true engines of wealth creation, namely their own brains, and can use new technology and partnerships to compete with companies a thousand times their own size, and win!

Case Study 4: diarymanager.com

Diarymanager.com is an Internet start-up that has survived and thrived despite the recent fall from favour of the dotcom companies. While there are many reasons for diarymanager.com's survival, including the fact that it has a sustainable business plan and has not overspent on advertising, the principal reason is its objective of partnering closely with all of its customers. And that means choosing customers carefully, ensuring that there will be mutual benefits of doing business that go beyond a simple exchange of services for cash. Why?

Because diarymanager.com intends to develop its service for many years to come, and the best way to do that is in collaboration with those who use it.

Diarymanager.com currently has four strategic partners: NTL, Flextech Interactive, iDesk and iTouch. They are all bigger companies and it is likely that this will always be the case. Diarymanager.com has no ambition to become a consumer brand and is committed to providing services on behalf of others. If we look at one of these partnerships – the one with NTL – we see that the lists of benefits for each partner is as follows:

Benefits to NTL

- an off-the-shelf, 'sticky application' that appears entirely under the NTL brand
- a small and flexible development partner that will bend over backwards to please
- access to the specialist expertise of the diarymanager.com team

Benefits to diarymanager.com

- association with a very well-known and respected brand
- opportunities for joint marketing and promotion
- direct access to the precise requirements of a market-leading Internet portal site

The example of diarymanager.com shows another important component in partnering, namely maximising the opportunity for specialisation. The great bureaucratic companies of the period from 1950 to 1990 look increasingly inappropriate for the commercial environment that is emerging in 2001. Before technology – particularly the Internet – allowed anyone to share any information with anyone else, very quickly, it was necessary for companies to build any function they wanted in house. Nowadays that simply doesn't make sense. Companies are increasingly going to outsource core functions and these provide multiple opportunities for smaller businesses to grow. Try to consider how your business could expand by providing outsourcing services to others in:

- finance
- personnel
- purchasing
- stock control
- maintenance contracting
- energy management . . .

There are thousands of other possible examples. To summarise, perhaps the best way to think of partnerships is as a key component in the restructuring of industry. What you do well, you can do for others. What others do well, they can do for you.

Making customers fall in love with you

It is a source of tremendous satisfaction to me that in *Design Week* magazine of 1993, Tony Key of BT described the Rufus Leonard approach to sales development as 'the best there is'. So what was so good about what we did?

As a new company starting out in the corporate design business, we were very aware that we did not necessarily know all we could know about design management. As design consultants we needed to be the experts, but how much experience did we really have regarding the global challenge of managing communications?

It occurred to me that all the real expertise was locked up in little silos inside giant companies. I hit upon the idea of inviting design managers from companies in for lunch, not to listen to us, but to talk about their own experiences. We were fortunate that the facility we shared with our parent company had a full-time cook, but the same output could have been achieved using an inexpensive restaurant.

As a first step I contacted the design manager from Shell, and asked if they would like to meet the design manager from BP. Having received an expression of interest, I then called the design manager of BP and asked if they would like to meet the design manager for Shell. Having got a yes from both of them, I invited the design manager of ICI to join. By this time, ICI were flattered to be invited to join such grand company.

Over lunch I made a point of listening, not talking. As I've said before, you sell with your ears, not your mouth. As the conversation among these global experts ebbed and flowed, we took careful notes and came to understand the secrets of best practice. We extended the seminars to include design managers from 33 companies, of which twenty were in the FTSE 100. The resulting body of research provided a unique resource to inform our sales development.

At the end of each seminar I asked the same question: 'If you were me, trying to sell to you, what would you do?'

I almost always got the same answer. These experts said there were 4,000 design companies in London, and they simply did not have time to sit through credential presentations from all of them. They said, in effect, 'Give us something useful, give us some research, then perhaps we will see you.'

It became apparent that, by running these seminars, we had developed a unique pool of research, and so that is what we eventually offered. When I sent a carefully prepared and checked mail-out to all the seminar participants, offering a presentation based on a synthesis of the seminar findings, the response was extraordinary. About one-third asked for a presentation, a 33 per cent response rate. Not what one expects from direct mail.

Over the following years we were invited to pitch for some enormous projects as a result of the seminars. In addition, we had a great resource to draw upon. Simply put, 33 of the most powerful design buyers in the UK owed us lunch. This was a great situation to be in. To give an example, one of our clients asked how best to launch their new corporate identity. To answer the question, I telephoned three of our seminar participants who had recently been through this process to ask how they did it. They each willingly spent five minutes on the telephone explaining, and at the end of the exercise we produced a pretty unique research report, based on global best practice, costing no more than a couple of lunches.

The seminar format had a life way beyond mere design management. As Rufus Leonard moved into electronic-media design, in 1996 we held another series of seminars, this time entitled 'Managing Communications in New Media'.

These were the early days of the Internet, and recruiting for the seminars could not have been easier. We were inundated with eager responses to our first mail-out on the subject. And exactly the same process followed: we rapidly gathered a world-class resource in how best to manage communications in new media.

So what are the lessons for building up smaller brands?

- Recognise that everyone likes to talk about their own job, even with competitors.
- The best way to sell is often to listen. If you understand your customers, they will respect you.
- Think how your company can aggregate real market expertise at low cost?
- Consider how to make what you do more interesting for your customers.
- How can you help your industry improve standards overall? If you are associated with that task, you are bound to benefit commercially.

The best proof I was ever given that we had struck gold with our seminar programme was when I interviewed someone for a job. I asked them how they had heard of Rufus Leonard. They said that when they started work at one of our much larger competitors, as part of their induction into the industry, they were told to read a copy of our corporate-identity seminar findings that they had obtained from a client.

Think about what your industry can learn more about, from itself. What strategies or forums can you use to bring people together? Whom would you buy lunch for, if you could? Remember, everyone hates being sold to, and dull presentations based on the idea that says 'We can help you because . . .' But everyone likes to talk, and share experiences outside of a sales environment. If you can develop an interesting environment to share ideas, the sales will come later, for sure.

Getting customers to stick

If you run any kind of facility, a great system for winning repeat business is to offer a free use of the facility at some point in the future in exchange for making a big booking today. This kind of incentive performs multiple functions:

- It rewards big-spending customers, who are likely to represent 80 per cent of your profits.
- It helps to get your facility scheduled into other people's diaries for advanced bookings.

> Through the provision of something free you enter into a deeper relationship with the customer.

Tie-ups to offer discounts can often be better presented as joint packages. Combining a discount or free offer for customers who use your hotel might be combined with partnerships in local car hire and restaurants. By individually offering something free or at cost price, a group of businesses in combination could show a prospective customer that they could get £200 to £600 in discount, if they book a two-week stay. In this way, what seems like a rather dull bonus scheme can become a powerful tool for attracting high-value customers.

The Social Venture Network

The president of the Social Venture Network (SVN) in America is a pioneering businesswoman who runs a restaurant called the White Dog Cafe (www.whitedog.com). Although it is just one restaurant it has an annual turnover of $5 million, and a huge reputation. She makes sure that she has visited all her suppliers, from meat and vegetables down to coffee. At a meeting of the European Social Venture Network I met Ben Cohen, the co-founder of Ben and Jerry's global ice-cream business. Unilever, the giant Anglo-Dutch cosmetics business, had just acquired his company, against his wishes. I asked him who would take over the mantle of pioneer in socially responsible business, and he suggested she would. (To find out more about her, and the Social Venture Network in general, see www.svneurope.com.)

The Social Venture Network was established in the USA and has grown and flourished there as well as starting in Europe and Asia. The heart of SVN is a core of very successful business people and high-net-worth individuals who are eager to make a positive change in society. They are eager to fund and develop businesses that address the environmental and social as well as financial agendas. Investment firms with names such as PYMWYMIC (Put Your Money Where Your Mouth Is Company, www.spop.de/Service/PYMWYMIC/pymwymic.html) and Extent (www.extent.nl), the investing operation of the Dutch multimillionaire Eckart Wintzen, are typical of this new breed of venture capitalists who believe that environmental and socially conscious businesses offer the greatest potential for the future.

Do you remember the Internet matchmaking event called 'First Tuesday'? It rapidly grew into a huge phenomenon. I attended one of the later meetings in May 2000. By this stage, Internet mania was just passing its peak. What characterised First Tuesday was the excess of entrepreneurs, and the shortage of venture capitalists. The investors, wearing lapel badges that identified them clearly, were surrounded by dotcom companies seeking funds. What is interesting about the Social Venture Network is that it represents the exact reverse of this phenomenon. The SVN conferences I attended in Holland and Sweden in 1999 and 2000 were characterised by great hordes of investors, and very few entrepreneurs. Maybe your business serves a social or environmental cause. If not, change your business so that it does. Then you can join SVN and start to collect some of the billions of dollars that are currently searching for social or environmental business opportunities.

Sustainable Responsible Investment

The movement away from great global businesses towards smaller, more sustainable companies operates at the highest level. The Sustainable Responsible Investment (SRI) movement is also called the Socially Responsible Investment movement, or sometimes the Ethical Investment movement. Funds managed ethically are well over $3 trillion dollars, and SRI funds are doubling every three years. To find out more about SRI look at the www.asria.org website. The founder of the ethical investment movement in Europe, Tessa Tennant, has set up AsriA to pioneer sustainable and responsible investment in the Asia region. The AsriA website offers leading-edge thinking from a world expert.

Currently, most of the world's large SRI funds are based on some measure of negative screening, avoiding questionable investments such as tobacco and gambling. Very little is currently invested in smaller business. But it will be. The opportunity exists for you to position your business as an alternative to the mainstream on either environmental or social grounds.

If you can demonstrate that you are part of the solution rather than the problem, huge amounts of capital can become available to build up your business. If this seems fanciful, notice that on 26 February 2001, the *Financial Times* launched an index of SRI funds in partnership with UNICEF, the United Nations children's charity. Blue-blooded American investment banks such as Merrill Lynch have launched funds investing in alternative-energy companies, with amounts of more than $200 million.

You may think your business could never compete in the alternative-energy market, but do you know what the appalling nightmare of climate change really means? It means we need:

- car sharing
- local food
- loft insulation
- double glazing
- low-energy light bulbs
- UK holidays

The biggest commercial opportunity in history

This is the era of globalisation, mass production, mass exports, imports, low cost, high volume, blah, blah, blah. But just remember that there are two interchangeable commodities that rule this new world. One is money, the other is time. And remember: they are interchangeable.

Look at LETS, or Local Exchange Trading Schemes. Flourishing across the UK and highly visible on the Internet (see www.gmlets.u-net.com), these fledgling enterprises are prototypes for many new varieties of company that manage to utilise information technology to manage trusting relationships between trustworthy people. To give an extreme example, isn't it ridiculous that we carry all our clothes away on holiday across the world, and others carry theirs over here. We stay in giant hotels at huge expense, when we could stay in one another's house essentially for free.

Local Exchange Trading Schemes try to keep wealth as far as possible inside a particular local area. The big idea is to swap things, and the value of these exchanges is recorded in a new monetary unit that normally has its own name. There are many different systems for managing these exchanges, but it is certainly true that the explosion of information technology makes them much easier to manage.

Partnerships in advertising

If a customer is giving you a lot of business, you should reward them. This simple, important principle is often forgotten by people. One of the best ways to celebrate your largest accounts is to buy advertising that promotes both your business and theirs. This approach is well developed in the fashion industry. A design label will usually reward its best customers by putting 2 per cent or more of the value of its annual order into advertising that promotes both the label and the shops that are selling it. In this way, the high-spending customers receive a benefit, which causes customers to spend more again – a virtuous circle.

There are many examples of this practice in big business. Did you realise, for example, that, when you hear the highly distinctive Intel sound inside an advert, this denotes that Intel have partially funded it? Or, when you see the usual two-page advert for Dixon's or Currys in tabloid newspapers, you may imagine that Currys or Dixon's paid for the adverts. This is not the case. The adverts are paid for by the manufacturers of electrical goods that appear within the advert.

Think hard about these advertising models. To what degree can you partner with other companies to produce combined promotions? The good of the many outnumbers and outguns the good of the few.

Copying the p.l.c. companies

It is usually the case that large, global companies will have supervisory boards, or boards of nonexecutive directors, who about once a month, or less often, take time to oversee the progress of a company and its board. The advantage of this system is that it gives those inside the company the opportunity to benefit from the wit and wisdom of seasoned business professionals from outside.

At a most basic level, it is good to have a formal board meeting structure where monthly you can discuss with colleagues and review:

- results
- cash flow/debtors
- monthly performance
- major changes in personnel or business activity
- projections
- proposed expenditure

Assuming your business has reached the level of maturity whereby you are running monthly meetings, it is useful to consider how your partners, or board of directors, might benefit from opening out discussions to a wider group. To give an example, if you run a nightclub, why not invite a local publican on to your board. As his premises shut, yours open, but you will both have many shared experiences regarding dealing with suppliers, unruly customers and attracting business. It was the famous management consultancy McKinsey & Company who first asserted the abiding truth that in almost every situation a team will exceed the capabilities of an individual.

This is perhaps the most fundamental lesson for a smaller business to learn as it grows. I know of a man who runs quite a successful small company, but he has real difficulty getting it to grow. He has worked hard, and in many ways he has suffered through his work. This has given him quite an inward and siege mentality, and this manifests itself in an inability to bring in new business partners as equals who can help grow the business.

Somebody new joining your decision-making group can improve its performance, be that group a board of directors or you sitting alone. Through discussion of different concepts, and different personalities talking about them, drawing on their own experience, a more rounded view will be reached. This principle has become enshrined in good-practice guidelines for larger companies in reports from Hample, Greenbury and others. But there is no reason why smaller companies cannot gain from similar policies. Remember also that business should be fun. What can be a more agreeable way to spend an evening than being involved in discussing your business with friends whose opinions you respect? New people coming into your business can bring both a new perspective and some of the enthusiasm for the enterprise that you first had when you started.

Businesses that go together like coffee and cream

There have been many revolutions in business, based on the principles of co-operation. One good example relates to the collaboration between different delivery organisations to carry each other's goods in empty vehicles. All that was required to build these partnerships was the acquisition of current data informing the companies of who had empty vehicles travelling from where to where. Once that data became available, competitor companies could bid to have their competitors manage the job at a steep discount, rather than send one of their own vehicles.

Such an approach can have significant difficulties in terms of organising insurance and other aspects of liability, but the benefits are huge. Specifically, twice the work gets done for the same amount of effort.

Examples of possible logical combinations include combining the duties of parking wardens with postal workers, or taxi companies with late-night shops. Why? Because parking wardens walk the streets, and so do postal delivery workers. Why combine taxi drivers and late-night shops? The idea would be to combine home delivery services with regular cab business, thereby increasing the utilisation of the cabs, and providing an alternative to the major supermarkets' home delivery.

Already there are brilliant examples of combined businesses, such as coffee shops inside booksellers', and ice-cream parlours inside cinemas. Think of the experience your customers go through. And think particularly of the journey they take to get what they want. Who might you be able to combine with effectively to achieve robust cross promotion?

Here are some areas to help you conceptualise:

- design companies with printers
- estate agents with solicitors
- hotels and restaurants
- non-UK companies who do the same thing
- Internet companies (share knowledge and software expertise)
- food shops and restaurants
- Thai food providers and pubs
- garages and fast-food outlets
- tailors and boutiques
- architects and interior designers
- crèches and shopping centres

Partnering with clients and customers

The tyranny of the television has robbed us very largely of any kind of social life on any kind of human scale. This is a lamentable loss, and it has even been suggested by the psychiatrist Mark Dickinson that humans watch soap operas to avoid depression that would otherwise accrue to us because we seldom talk or communicate socially any more.

Smaller businesses have huge potential to fill that social deficit. There are a thousand ways a smaller business can build community with employees, customers and suppliers. Examples include:

- organising five-a-side football games
- running book clubs, where novels are collectively read and then discussed
- holding parties – it's surprising how inexpensive it can be to hold a small get-together, and yet this is a great resource; you can even make it a weekly or monthly fixture
- establishing games and quiz nights
- weekends away in the country (to hire a cottage or series of cottages is relatively inexpensive in some parts of the UK)
- organising country walks
- inviting members of your company community to give short talks on subjects of their choosing

This last example can be extremely effective indeed. The design company Newel and Sorrell, now part of Interbrand, had delightful offices in London's Primrose Hill in an annexe called Utopia Village. There they held a series of talks aptly named 'Utopian Nights'. This successful series involved persuading some interesting, but not necessarily very famous, speakers to come and address an audience of employees, clients and friends on a subject of general interest. The talks were recorded and subsequently issued in a book that was both interesting in its own right, and helped build the brand of the company.

CHAPTER NINE

Developing innovative positioning

Chapter outline

In this chapter, we look at evaluating how to turn what you do into a more coherent and attractive package. We look at responsible retailing, and give four case studies, then examine the four Ds of effective positioning.

Breaking the mould

Retailers with names such as 'Just Sausages' are building compelling experiences by tapping consumer demand for quality and choice using organic local ingredients and putting the fun back into shopping.

A good approach for consideration of innovative positioning is to review the strategies of some brilliantly innovative larger companies that have fused logic and creativity to break the mould of conventional commerce. These companies are true thought leaders, described well by Peter Kellner in his paper written for The Co-operative Party, *New Mutualism, The Third Way*:

> The American political scientist, Robert Axelrod, has used computer simulations to develop game theory, and showed how sophisticated 'trust' strategies have a greater chance of success than those that employ no trust at all. Diplomacy works best when there is trust: the Northern Ireland peace process provides

a dramatic example of this. And modern business theory asserts that trust-relationships, both within and between firms, generally work better than relationships based solely on formal contracts.

Case Study: Johnson & Johnson

Doing well by doing good

As long ago as 1943, Johnson & Johnson, the American-owned manufacturer of healthcare products ranging from drugs to Band-Aid, published a 'credo' that put customers first, employees second, the community third and shareholders fourth. At the time the company was still run by the Johnson family, and could set its priorities without fearing a backlash from external shareholders. However, the credo has survived Johnson & Johnson's growth into one of the world's largest healthcare companies, worth $100 billion, employing 91,000 people and operating in 175 countries throughout the world.

Johnson & Johnson's credo

1 We believe our first responsibility is to the doctors, nurses and patients, to mothers and fathers and all others who use our products and services. In meeting their needs everything we must do must be of high quality. We must constantly strive to reduce our costs in order to maintain reasonable prices. Customers' orders must be serviced promptly and accurately. Our suppliers and distributors must have an opportunity to make a fair profit.

2 We are responsible to our employees, the men and women who work with us throughout the world. Everyone must be considered as an individual. We must respect their dignity and recognise their merit. They must have a sense of security in their jobs. Compensation must be fair and adequate, and working conditions clean, orderly and safe. We must be mindful of ways to help our employees fulfil their family responsibilities. Employees must feel free to make suggestions and complaints. There must be equal opportunity for employment, development and advancement for those qualified. We must provide competent management, and their actions must be just and ethical.

3 We are responsible to the communities in which we live and work and to the world community as well. We must be good citizens – support good works and charities and bear our fair

share of taxes. We must encourage civic improvements and better health and education. We must maintain in good order the property we are privileged to use, protecting the environment and natural resources.

4 Our final responsibility is to our stockholders. Business must make a sound profit. We must experiment with new ideas. Research must be carried on, innovative programs developed and mistakes paid for. New equipment must be purchased, new facilities provided and new products launched. Reserves must be created to provide for adverse times. When we operate according to these principles, the stockholders should realise a fair return.

Case Study: B&Q

Green policies are good for business

B&Q, the UK's largest hardware and do-it-yourself retail chain, decided that, from the end of 1999, it would buy timber only from independently certified sources. This policy is designed to help the world's forests, by ensuring that no timber bought by B&Q results from harmful deforestation. It is part of a strategy to persuade the company's suppliers to adopt environmentally friendly practices. In 1993 B&Q stopped buying any mahogany from Brazil.

Following criticism in 1990 from Friends of the Earth, B&Q initiated a Supplier Environmental Audit (or SEA). It found that fewer than half its suppliers had any kind of pro-environmental policy, and only 8 per cent had a policy that 'demonstrated understanding and commitment'. As a result, B&Q investigated each of its suppliers and awarded it a ranking from A (excellent) to F (fail). In December 1993 only 35 per cent were rated C or above. The remaining companies were warned that B&Q would stop buying from them if they did not achieve a C rating, or better, by the end of 1994.

All bar 6 per cent of suppliers reached this target; ten companies were delisted; another 19 were given a final chance to reach C grade, and did so. In 1995 B&Q merged its quality and environmental departments, and established a ten-point 'QUEST' code for its suppliers (QUEST: 'The Quality of a product includes its Ethics and SafeTy'). Five of the ten points cover environmental issues, the other five quality issues. The company then insisted that all suppliers achieve a B rating by the end of 1999. B&Q's strategy shows that, even without legislation, it is possible for a large company in a highly competitive market to adopt tough pro-environment policies, induce similar policies among its suppliers, and still prosper.

Through mutual understanding and trust, smaller businesses can collaborate to achieve equally impressive positioning and goals. The opportunity for a renaissance in smaller business is to build bigger brands by collaborating around common goals.

Case study: The Co-operative Bank

Profits through principles

In 1998 the Co-operative Bank sought to reconnect itself with mutual values by developing a new mission statement applying co-operative principles to the modern world of financial services. The bank's ethical policy had already been operating since 1992, following a major consultation exercise to find out what customers felt about how the bank should invest their money – and how it shouldn't.

All new business-customer applications are screened against a strict set of ethical criteria, with complex decisions referred to an ethical policy unit. Out of the companies referred to the unit, 23 per cent have been found to fall short of customers' standards. In some of these cases, the bank has been able to help the customer in question to resolve the conflict with the policy and come on board. Turning away business is never easy, but, under the ethical policy, that is precisely what the bank has done whenever it has come across a customer unable or unwilling to comply with it. In 1997 the bank launched its Partnership Approach to business, identifying seven partners who are crucial to its business success. These partners are

1 shareholders
2 customers
3 staff and their families
4 suppliers
5 local community
6 national and international societies
7 past and future generations of co-operators

It polled 1.2 million customer households to determine their support for the bank's new definition of its responsibilities. A hundred thousand customers responded, with 97 per cent backing the Partnership Approach. Subsequently the bank published its 'warts-and-all' Partnership Report, which assesses how it delivers value to these seven groups. It also assesses whether value has been met in a socially responsible and ecologically sustainable manner.

Far from having an adverse effect on profits, this policy has seen the bank enjoy rising profits over the preceding four years, culminating in a record £55 million. The bank also makes positive cash contributions to enterprises and organisations whose activities reflect the concerns and wishes of customers, ensuring as many mutual outcomes as possible in an unlikely industry.

Case Study: Co-operative Wholesale Society (CWS)

A responsible retailer

CWS Retail's 'Responsible Retailing' policy is a modern expression of the principles set out by the founders of the modern co-operative movement. A Gallup survey carried out on CWS's behalf in 1995 sought to judge the public mood on ethical issues such as animal welfare, the environment, care for the community, product labelling and human rights. It showed that customers are ready and willing to penalise retailers and products that fail to meet their ethical standards, and reward those that do. The survey findings revealed a public conviction that retailers and manufacturers are not giving customers the full facts about the goods and services they provide. While customers are anxious to use their spending power responsibly, they do not believe that retailers are on their side – and are wary of environmental and ethical claims made by the food industry to the contrary.

In response, the CWS since 1995 has introduced new policies in the following areas:

Labelling

Clear and honest labelling – CWS identifies 'tricks of the trade' that are used to make products sound bigger and better than they really are, producing a code of practice and calling for the industry to adhere to it.

Animal welfare

CWS launches 'Ending the Pain' – a campaign against animal testing in the toiletries industry.

Fair trade
CWS commits to joining the Ethical Trading Initiative (ETI), building partnerships to improve conditions of workers worldwide. CWS 99 Tea brand becomes the first mainstream food product to incorporate ethical sourcing criteria.

Diet and health
CWS leads the industry by providing sensible drinking advice on its wines and spirits. CWS is the first retailer to announce a ban on the sale of 'alcopops' in its stores. Having suffered from the poor image of 'the Co-op' and lost market share to the likes of Tesco, Sainsbury, Safeway and Asda, CWS is still the market leader in convenience stores (often in remote areas) and responsible retailing is leading to increased sales. Take-up of their Dividend Card now stands at about one and three-quarter million, and rising. Now, CWS is an organisation at the heart of the UK co-operative movement with sales of more than £3 billion. Owner of The Co-operative Bank and the Co-operative Insurance Society, CWS is the largest Co-operative retailer in Europe, the UK's largest farmer and employs nearly 40,000 people.

Grabbing attention

Most business is very boring. How can you combine ethics with business to grab the media's attention? Politics combined with business is intrinsically interesting and therefore newsworthy, and that equals free publicity for your business.

A brilliant example of how to combine a smaller business with politics to create a huge impression in the media comes from Katharine Hamnett, the fashion designer. As a plucky smaller business, she was invited with others to a press reception at 10 Downing Street. In front of the cameras she took off her coat and shook hands with Prime Minister Margaret Thatcher, wearing a T-shirt emblazoned with the following slogan in huge letters: '58% SAY NO TO PERSHING'.

This was a reference to the proposed establishment of US missiles in Europe, a policy Margaret Thatcher endorsed. So what happened? The resulting photo became the most used press photo in the world that year. The publicity value that accrued to Hamnett was worth many millions of pounds. So the lesson is, if you can combine politics with business, you are on to a sure-fire winner.

Think about the strategies and positioning developed by these major companies. Can you find a way that your business could develop a high-profile image and identity as an ethical or environmentally responsible concern. How can you position yourself to connect with the future of commerce, and thereby gain customers from the morally bankrupt, environmentally irresponsible traditional big businesses?

If you are a smaller player in your market, then probably the best way to succeed is to distinguish your offering by making it unique and relevant to a particular audience. Dominant businesses may be rather bland and not cater properly for smaller but extremely lucrative niche markets. Success in a niche market can be developed, over time, into success in a wider marketplace.

Four goals for effective positioning

In an article for the *Financial Times*'s 'Mastering Marketing' series last year, Alice M Tybout and Brian Sternthan identify 'four Ds of effective positioning':

1 brand definition
2 clear differentiation
3 deepening of the brand's connection with customer goals over time
4 defence of the brand position as competitors challenge it and customer tastes change.

Let's examine these four goals with particular reference to smaller businesses. Think about your product or service and try listing its defining and differentiating features. Think about your target market: what innovations could you introduce to improve the position of your product or service in the market?

Definition and differentiation

Tybout and Sternthan describe the mechanism by which brands need to claim membership of a product type, say washing liquid, but then also differentiate the particular brand from other products in that category, like the Ecover brand, for instance, by being environmentally friendly. For smaller brands it is this dual process of claiming membership and differentiation that is important:

> Smaller brands typically claim parity on the category-defining benefit to establish membership and focus on some secondary category feature as their point of difference. Accordingly, IBM emphasises state-of-the-art technology as its point of difference, whereas laptop maker WinBook claims that it delivers state-of-the-art technology at a lower price.

I recently worked with a start-up company that aims to establish itself in the network equipment technology market. With large companies, in particular Cisco Systems, dominating the market, the company needed to define its brand carefully as a part of that market, but also to differentiate itself by highlighting specialist features that the market leaders were less focused on but for which their target customers had a clear requirement.

A large part of both the definition and differentiation of a brand is about the language you use to describe your product or service. Palm, the hand-held-computer maker, has used the expression 'personal organiser' to define its product as part of the category that Filofax had established. Text messaging became popular only once people could understand what is was: SMS (Short Messaging Service) has been around for a long time, but users started to realise what this was only when the networks started to call SMS messages 'text' messages. Text messages were defined as being similar to email, but different because they can be sent and received from any mobile telephone.

Rufus Leonard, the corporate-identity consultancy, is easily defined as being a design company. But, with so many design companies out there, an early point of differentiation for it was that it worked exclusively for FTSE 100 companies. The Co-operative Bank is like any other high street bank, but smaller. The bank has developed a very strong brand through the differentiation of having a strong ethical policy

The areas of definition and differentiation for your brand are not superficial. As with the other two Ds of effective positioning, these are strategic rather than cosmetic decisions. The positioning you choose is fundamental to what your business is and does.

Is your product or service category clearly defined? What makes your product or service different? Be careful not to create a confusing message by having too many differentiating features. Keep it simple. Less is often more.

Have you identified exactly who will be choosing to use your product or service? Are you sure that your differentiators are important to these decision-makers? Are they realistic and believable? What else do you know about your target customers and their wider goals and objectives?

Deepening your brand

To deepen your brand you need to know as much as possible about your potential customers – not only their specific requirements but also their broader goals and objectives. Now that you have defined clearly your brand's points of definition and differentiation, successful positioning in the market requires this 'deepening' of your position.

Deepening your brand position is about making the link between the specific product or service you offer and your customers' wider goals. It is also about the relationships of dependability and trust discussed in Chapter 6. Tybout and Sternthan use the concept of a 'ladder', which connects the specific features of a product with the wider, more abstract 'brand values', which then connect with the goals and aspirations of customers. They describe how McDonald's has 'laddered up from the cleanliness of its restaurants and the good taste of its food, to a place that was good for kids, to a trusted place in the community'.

Rufus Leonard has achieved this by creating a studio that reflects the creativity of the company's product. It positions its services to its clients as creative and valuable, and, when clients come into the studio, the physical environment they find themselves in is relaxing but with remarkable attention to detail and a pleasing creative energy. For many clients this is the kind of place they would like to have as their office, an experience that connects the actual service that is being provided to them with their own wider aspirations.

Defending your brand

Even if your business is well established you will need to keep your brand positioning and its relationship with your customers' goals under continual review. This is especially the case when you are a smaller business competing against larger more powerful companies. You may need to use the nimble, flexible characteristics of a smaller business to subtly position and reposition your products and services. Your established, trusting customer relationships are of vital importance, and you must devise strategies for continually deepening the relationship your customers have with you and your brand.

Once this is established, do not be too radical about changing your position. If your innovation is successful in the market, others will copy it. But it may be that this will serve to reinforce your position as the leader in the field. Ikea never sue a competitor for copying their designs. Instead they see it as a spur to design something even better. At the same time you need to actively develop and introduce new features because, if you don't, your competitors will. And it is at that point that your product is under threat.

Hoover and Electrolux were not interested in vacuum cleaners that had no dust bags because the sale of dust bags for their appliances was a reasonable revenue stream for them. But by ignoring Dyson's innovation they have lost market share. If they had simply introduced a similar feature in their own product lines, Dyson would likely not be in the successful position it is in today. Dyson succeeded by having a simple differentiator: a vacuum cleaner that doesn't need a bag. The slow response of the incumbent brands in this category means that, if Hoover or Electrolux were to market a similar product, they would be promoting a feature that consumers may associate with Dyson rather than Hoover or Electrolux. New financial products that combine your mortgage, current account, savings and credit cards could be introduced by any bank, but consumers may well describe these products as 'a bit like the Virgin One account', thus reinforcing the original innovator's brand.

Schweppes, the soft-drinks company, used to have a slogan that ran, 'Schh, you know who . . .' A competitor with a longer pedigree than Schweppes ran an advertising campaign with the clever slogan, 'We knew how before you know who'. Unfortunately, market research revealed that the public mistook this advert for a Schweppes advert. So the first-mover advantage is of particular relevance here. If you innovate well, you dominate.

Innovation is about imagining the future, not stirring up the past. Design guru Jamie Anley of the design company Jam has said that market research is like trying to use the rear-view mirrors to combat snow on the windscreen. A BBC annual report once observed that nobody had ever written in to the corporation to request a situation comedy about a rag-and-bone man and his father, yet *Steptoe and Son* was hugely popular.

Checklist for brand innovation

- Are you keeping a careful watch on your competitors?
- Do they have an innovation that you can emulate before they can establish ownership of it in the market?
- Do you have a strong differentiator that you can use to establish your product or service quickly as better than the products of your larger competitors?
- How would you know if your customers' tastes or preferences are changing?

Waste not . . .

It is a good use of any entrepreneur's time to look at the highly successful importer of Japanese goods called Muji. One of the biggest ideas behind the Muji brand is that there is no waste. Packaging at Muji is sparse and functional, and that tells the consumer that most of the costs of the goods have been expended on the goods themselves rather than lavish packaging.

Not having any branding is the essence of the Muji magic. There is in fact no real excuse for elaborate packaging that fails to achieve anything in its own right. If you make packaging that is big and durable, make sure it can serve a useful purpose after it has been got rid of. The Body Shop process of reusing plastic bottles serves a variety of objectives:

- builds a closer relationship with customers
- makes customers feel good about themselves
- saves money on packaging
- saves waste and consequently damage to the environment
- does something no other retailer is doing

It is this last point that defines the opportunity for every smaller brand that wants to make it big. Don't follow: lead.

Shop blindness

There is a problem that can blight retailers, called 'shop blindness', and inside this specific problem lies a lesson that can be applied to much wider groups of businesses. The problem is this: a product will be selling well in a particular part of a shop, perhaps for years, and then suddenly it will fail. Sales will plummet and nobody will be able to tell why.

Normally the answer to the mystery is that something small but important has gone wrong. Perhaps the display has been moved, or a doorway has been closed, changing the routing customers use to pass the display. The crucial point is that this problem is invisible to the staff in the shop. They have become 'shop blind', being in the same place, month after month, year after year.

The solution to shop blindness, as in so many other areas of business, is to get a second, or third, opinion. Try to make sure that as many people from outside the business as possible can comment regularly on what you are doing well, or badly. Many heads are better than one.

Preparing for the future

Our society has to change dramatically. As we have seen already, numerous environmental crises threaten our very existence. There are many necessary responses to this problem. One of the major ones will certainly be a migration from value-added tax to value-extracted tax. If you understand why this is going to happen, you will be in a better position to develop a proposition that is better suited to the future environment.

For 2,000 years governments have taxed completely the wrong thing. They have taxed what is clearly very abundant, namely labour. They have failed to tax what is very scarce, namely the use of natural resources.

The net result of this is some ludicrous distortions in society. Examples include the fact that there are often many millions without jobs, but, when you telephone any business, usually a very user-unfriendly computer answering service will take you to voicemail, no matter how simple and quick your question might be. Another example of this idiocy can be seen when you break a car headlight. Typically just one piece of glass needs replacing, but a headlight bulb unit may well contain thirty or more components, all stuck together. When you buy a new bulb, you will buy all thirty components, stuck together, and throw all the old bulb away.

Remember that all that needed replacing was one piece of glass. To do the task manually, assuming you're competent to do so, might take and hour or two. Because we tax labour so highly, this is 'too expensive'. So we buy a whole new light unit, made by machine, because the resources are not taxed.

Boards of directors are very good at avoiding tax. If you tax something, they will stop doing it. For this reason, politicians in the near future will start shifting taxes from value-added to value-extracted.

So what will happen when that change starts to occur? Well, typically, we will move to more sane and sustainable means of transport. And what does that mean? Well, for one thing, the car of the future is undoubtedly the Citroën 2CV. It has very low fuel consumption, and all parts are readily replaceable. So how will the appetites of wealthy people be satisfied in this egalitarian world of the 2CV? There will simply be many more models, along the following lines:

- The bottom-of-the-range model will be a standard car.
- The next upgrade will be a 2CV where the car is checked and washed for you once a month.
- The next-best car in the series will be checked and cleaned once each week, or day.
- The next upgrade will have a chauffeur who drives you anywhere by day.
- The next upgrade will have you driven 24 hours per day.
- The top-of-the-range car will be painted by a famous artist.

In this way we can continue with the concept of wealth and luxury, but move to a sustainable society. If this outcome seems fanciful, bear in mind we have no choice whatsoever but to change completely. This will all happen soon, simply because it has to.

So how can you develop your business so it is more effectively optimised for the new economic environment? You need to try to consider businesses that make more use of labour as a substitute for scarce environmental resources. Consider expanding your business to include:

- car share with chauffeur service
- home delivery
- exotic cooking with UK ingredients
- vehicle (and other) repair services

- luxury-service UK holidays
- home heating and insulation management services
- factory and manufacturing redesign for reduced energy use

It has been said that leadership is a simple matter of working out where everyone is going, running ahead of them and shouting 'Over here' at the top of your voice. Think about the changes we are soon to experience in terms of taxes and benefits relating to manufacture, and develop business positioning that can best optimise the opportunities.

CHAPTER TEN

Developing a culture that thinks big

Chapter outline

In this chapter I look at how to develop a consistent and healthy culture in your business. A massive ingredient of culture is language, so the chapter finishes off with some practical tips on language. The right words will strengthen every aspect of your brand. It's nearly time for some action! You have all but one of the essential ingredients for your company's killer application: identity.

Components of identity

Your brand is created and reinforced by everything that your business does: every phone call you answer or make, every letter or email you write, every visit anyone makes to your workplace, every contact anyone has with your product. You have worked out your brand positioning and developed strategies for promoting your business through partnerships. You have thought about how to build and maintain trust with your customers and about their perceptions of your business. You have considered what branding is and what you can achieve through developing your brand.

Wally Olins is the father of corporate identity. He was the first to articulate the concept as the result of all impressions that the organisation makes on its employees, customers, and everyone who interacts with it. Components of identity include all products and services your organisation provides, the work environment, offices, class-rooms, stores, and information in all media about your services and products. Crucially, corporate identity includes the culture of your business. That is, the way you interact with employees, clients and partners.

If your culture thinks big it must be a big step nearer to actually being big. It is the greatest possible art to think, seriously, about doing things on a more significant scale than your competitors. Think about the culture of your business, reflected in things such as inside jokes, informal slogans, rituals, myths, beliefs, values and, of course, language.

> ■ What would you say characterises the culture of your business? Think of ten words you could use to describe your company.
>
> ■ What is important to people in your company? What type of behaviour gets rewarded?
>
> ■ Which of these characteristics are important to your customer relationships?
>
> ■ Which of these characteristics are important to your staff?
>
> ■ Which of these characteristics could be damaging to your brand?

No makeover or strategy consultant can develop a consistent and healthy culture in your business. Your company culture is the result of consistently skilful leadership. A healthy company culture stems from those at the top of an organisation or business working in a way that motivates and values people.

It is the wise manager who knows that by far the company's most valuable asset goes up and down in the elevator each day: the people. Your business culture must work with all the other, material, aspects of your identity so that your staff are proud of their company and their work, and have only good things to say about the business. At the bus stop, at a party or in the gym your people must, without pre-tence, be talking up your brand and proudly giving people their business cards.

Here are some things you should consider to help you to build a healthy company culture:

> ■ **Communicate your business strategy clearly to everyone in the company**. Absolutely everyone needs to understand what their company is all about, what products and services it sells, who its

customers are, who the competition are in the marketplace and why your company is better than them. These things need to make sense to everyone, and the underlying logic of your strategy must fit well with their values. If your people don't agree with your strategy you need to know why not.

- **Let people be different**. There is no way that a business that does not allow people to have and express their own personalities will be a happy place. Encourage creativity in your business and let people take more control of how they are going to help to build success. Results, not dull routine.

- **Give people space**. With space comes creativity and innovation, with rules and regulations come frustration and unhappiness. Of course you need to make sure people are on your side, but, if you make them turn up at 9, expect them to leave at 5. Let them turn in when they're ready to get the job done and they won't leave until they have.

- **Use words carefully**. Language is at the heart of all culture. NTL do not have 'employees', rather 'associates'; AOL does not have 'customers' but 'members'; Disney employees are 'hosts' and their customers are 'guests'.

Mind your language

Language is probably the best tool you have for building a bigger brand. The words you use help to define the culture of your company and as you use the Internet in your business these words will travel globally.

- How are the words you use in your business applied in your products and services?
- How are they used in your buildings, offices or shops?
- How do your staff use them?
- What words do you use in your marketing materials, both in print and on the Internet?

To be effective with language, keep it brief. People today have less time to linger over what they read. Make everything you write less bulky and more relevant. Your customers want the information quickly. Take great pains over making every word as plain and as intelligible as possible.

- Keep language relevant.
- Don't waffle.
- Distil everything down to its essence without losing all personality.
- Make it easy but not patronising.

The Internet and language

Your business and your brand have access to the entire English-speaking world. More significantly, perhaps, the entire English-speaking world can have access to your business. The Internet facilitates this.

The lower overheads and the lack of any physical barriers to competition mean that smaller companies using the Internet are much better placed to make a real go of offering their products and services to a wide range of people. In the past, small companies could not achieve the reach afforded to large corporations with their chains of expensive physical outlets across a large area and their high-budget marketing campaigns.

On the Internet, each company has a similar potential reach, no matter how large or small it is. Advertising can be much more targeted and less expensive. The Internet allows customers to go out searching for services in a way they were never able to do previously. If you have something that people will genuinely want, you do not have to be big to create a big brand and – as far as your customers are concerned – a big company.

Talking to your customers

Always be clear and direct. Using the Internet means that your customers, old and new, have enormous choice. They are less and less afraid to use it. If you waffle or present stodgy copy, then what does that say about your business?

Develop a written personality for your brand and stick to it. Make sure the personality is real for you. But be clear about your personality and develop a style and tone to match. Be modern. Very traditional, bureaucratic copy is hardly ever appropriate. The Internet enables your brand to become a part of a global conversation, so be careful to choose a language that fits all.

The Internet revolution is certainly changing language. It is inevitable. All websites are the same size, and offer the same basic functionality. So, in that environment, language becomes pivotal. Because the Internet is driven by immediacy, and people are sick of the slow speed it sometimes operates at – the 'World Wide Wait' – language on the Web has to perform more, and faster. If it is stodgy or boastful, you will lose people.

People travel less when using the Web, but they actually do more. They book hotels and flights, buy books and track deliveries. And with this increased convenience come expectations about speed, simplicity and general ease of use. In response, language needs to become briefer. That need not mean fewer words overall, but each item will need to be shorter and more incisive. Try to distil every phrase down to its essence, but still keep the tone of voice that fits with your corporate identity. Make communications very easy to understand, but be careful not to go to extremes. Don't be patronising.

The speed at which customers deal with your website is critical. Some 50 per cent of online transactions are not completed simply because customers tire of all the form filling. They do not have the patience. The trick is to remove anecdotes and other waffle, and to become more focused. Communicating an instant meaning is the key. Never be oblique.

The Internet can address an audience of more than one billion people with some basic command of English. It has been suggested that there are more people studying English in China than there are speaking it in the rest of the world. To write for an audience where English may not be the first language requires a particular approach. Things to avoid are:

- unnecessary jargon
- overcomplex or particularly rare or obscure words
- national jokes that could be taken the wrong way
- very idiomatic phrasing and peculiarly British metaphors

Alternatively, you might decide that the reverse is true. If your website offers software services particularly aimed at computer games developers, you can adopt that whole language and way of communicating, knowing that, from Boston to Bangalore, a games developer has a vocabulary and common interest, whatever their nation or culture might be.

The trick is to be absolutely clear about what your language is aiming to achieve, and write with that at the forefront of your mind, stopping now and then to read it as your intended audience might. Always subject it to a second, or third, pair of eyes before you upload it to your website.

To cajole and persuade on the Internet, it is vital to adopt a less dictatorial tone and to be more pleasantly seductive and persuasive. Be polite and encourage interaction and email suggestions. Words from customers can make you a smarter organisation.

The Internet user is generally a highly independent and self-directed soul. You will need to reflect these character traits and find the right tone of voice to fit with them. Avoid obscure or condescending word forms. To master the correct tone of voice, try to consider what your prospective customer is really like. When describing a sales pitch that was to be made recently, I described the buyer as American, 55 years old, worth perhaps $10 million, but did not consider himself wealthy. Now this exact person does not in fact exist, but I was conjuring up an image of him to help frame the development of the most appropriate language. This process will help you consider which words and ideas are appropriate, and which are not.

Brand values

Making sure that your copy reflects your brand values is important. It's as well to write down a list of those values – if you haven't already got a statement of them printed and available to your staff. But don't worry if you haven't: the concept of brand values – developed by larger companies to achieve consistency – is just a statement of what you are like. So write down and discuss with colleagues what you are really about. Think of a few words or phrases that really capture the best aspects of your business. That might mean friendly, accessible, flexible and fun; or it might mean professional, exact, detailed and thorough.

There should be something unique and good in the brand values you write down. Try to capture the essence of your organisation, and immortalise that in a few words. You can then use those words to judge the way your written communications work. Do they match your brand values? Are you talking to people the way you want to?

Having got the tone of voice right, make sure all your communications follow this style. Although the Web demands certain particular aspects to writing, the overall impression of your company, in printed literature, on the Web and even in letters and reports, should be as consistent as possible. In essence, this is about seeming co-ordinated and organised rather than fragmented and confused.

In terms of style in communications, it is a good idea to be as natural as possible, and of course honest. If you try to oversell it can seem foolish. So try not to state that products are 'incredible' or 'astounding'. Remember also that your prices may well not be 'unbeatable'. Anyway, people have heard this hackneyed sales talk so many times they are probably completely sick of it.

Flow and connection

A good test of your ability to write effective communications is to assess how well the words flow. Try reading what you have written out loud. Does it sound natural? In Chapter 5, I cautioned against use of the passive voice. There is no harm in repeating that advice here. To make sure you relate to people in a way that seems human, it is better to choose the active voice, which also allows you to incorporate those vital words 'we' and 'you'. So don't say 'will be sent' or 'can be used', but 'we will send', 'you can use'. A good test of succinctness is to try to write everything you want, then halve the number of words you have used and rewrite accordingly. At the extreme, the famous wit and lexicographer Samuel Johnson wrote that you should read through what you have written, and, wherever you see a phrase you are particularly proud of, strike it out!

When writing for a website, start off by making a structure chart showing all the different information that you want to present. Then make sure the homepage carries an effective index of these components. In any medium, make sure headings are really relevant. People do not read everything they see these days. It is likely they will skip through and navigate using headings. Make sure that your signposts are relevant and appropriate.

What do customers care about?

Sustainability Product Marketing (SPM)

Managers need to build simple, easy-to-implement strategies that achieve competitive corporate advantage by:

- recognising that without using care, business leaders will never build trust with employees or customers
- acknowledging the environment and the sustainability crisis while rejecting values-free business strategies
- acknowledging employees as humans and not farm animals capable of giving only in proportion to what they receive; see them in broader terms than the mere financial
- acknowledging customers as intelligent, averse to condescending, low-quality or mundane communications, desirous of rich experiences and searching for answers to complex problems
- trying to raise the tone a little – life is too short for the volumes of banal consumption we are currently chalking up at accelerating speeds

This fourth point is worth elaborating upon a little. The era of values-free, overconsumption capitalism, with its cancerous vortex of 'work harder, buy more', is coming to an end. The successful twenty-first-century manager will have to learn to migrate from the Muzak economy of the shopping centre to the Mozart economy of mass customisation and a richer quality of life.

The business of business is business . . .

. . . And it has nothing to do with pollution, the environment or whatever. Do you agree? Let us think of business ethics and the commercial opportunities presented by the sustainability crisis.

It is impressive to see the many movements made by corporations to become more responsible in their operations and activities. However, establishing a social conscience, philanthropy and so forth is an insufficiently radical response to the very substantial threats faced by our planet and species.

We should also understand that we got into this mess with business and technology, and it will be business and technology that will be needed to get us out again. In the words of James Lovelock, 'We cannot solve the problem through a reactionary, back to nature campaign because we are so integrally part of the technosphere it would be like jumping off a liner in the middle of the ocean to swim the rest of the journey in glorious independence.'

But only small businesses have the intellectual resources to save the day. Big companies are imprisoned in a system that chains them. To give an example, a leading company, much admired in this field, is J Sainsbury p.l.c., the £13.5 billion retailer of food and other products. Sainsbury's have shown some measure of commitment to resolving the climate-change problem through the development of solar cooling systems for lorries, and advanced power-reduction systems for offices. This is all to be applauded. But it fails to address two key areas where CO_2 emissions are at their most severe and damaging: in food production and distribution. Sainsbury's simply cannot realistically substitute anything for CO_2 produced by distribution vehicles. And to try to persuade suppliers to emit less CO_2 would almost inevitably result in a raising of prices, and contraction of the range of goods on offer.

So, for Sainsbury's, climate change is an issue that they would like to respond to, but cannot. This unfortunate bind restricts the activities of more than 95 per cent of the world's larger corporations: they cannot respond to the dreadful threat.

There are, however, alternatives for every possible avenue of expenditure. Small businesses can triumph in these areas. Here are some organisations that can profit through reduced CO_2 emissions:

- Videoconference, telecommunications. Rationale: alternative to travel. The videoconference company Eye-Network.com makes a lot of money by taking the most profitable business from the world's airlines.

- Travel companies using sailing ships. Rationale: alternative to unsustainable air transport. If this seems improbable, bear in mind that air fuel is not taxed, yet, but has in any case doubled in price during 2000 to around 7% of airline costs. Expect legislation to double it a few more times, and the idea of a long cruise on a computer-controlled sailing ship becomes very attractive.

- Home insulation companies. Rationale: alternative to heating. Double-glazing and loft-insulation companies take note! Your country needs you like never before.

- Local food production. Rationale: alternative to food travel (statistics from the Soil Association show that food travels an average of 2,000 miles to our dinner tables).

- Art, culture and entertainment online. Rationale: 'dematerialised' products and services require small expenditure of energy to produce and transmit.

For each problem faced by our species, there is a particular opportunity for smaller businesses to demolish bigger ones. So we can sum up the essential rationale behind SPM with these observations:

1 The ecosystems that keep the earth safe for humans are quite robust, or else they would have failed by now.

2 They are in imminent danger of failing because various bigger businesses have developed outputs that are so vast as to threaten nature's capacity to absorb toxins.

3 The vast bulk of industrial systems are now controlled by the behaviour of supranational companies, which are causing such substantial impacts by their activities that the biosphere itself is threatened.

4 The demand for these resource-heavy products is so widespread and popular as to defy political action – look at car use.

5 Because they are so large, it is probable that substantial financial sums are being directed towards these unsustainable activities.

6 Given that for every form of expenditure there is an alternative, and the larger the market, the greater the incentive to substitute, it follows that alternatives to unsustainable industries should promote themselves as such.

7 In practical effect, this means that small businesses should become actively political through their marketing, and adverts should be created that absolutely terrify the general public. There are good reasons to be terrified, and the public should be told of the risks we face.

8 Markets and advertising have been allowed to develop substantial and sophisticated mechanisms for allowing the public to select the best-'value' product in terms of price and quality. However, with the notable exception of cigarettes and asbestos, there has been little effort expended to limit or discourage damaging products.

9 It will probably prove politically unacceptable for governments to deliver the bad news of the sustainability crisis to the public. However, it should not cost government to allow, and even encourage, smaller businesses to market products and services that increase the chances of human survival. Indeed, it is generally agreed by political thinkers of both the right and left

that direct state intervention in the economy is undesirable. To permit the full and proper exploitation of local markets and marketing mechanisms for both the individual and common good is both acceptable and desirable.

10 Smaller businesses are poised to capitalise on the backlash away from multinational companies.

Business and justice

You do not have to be a placard-waving environmental anarchist to know that our world is in more than a spot of bother. The supreme issue is climate change, and any aspect of your business that can leverage the innate advantages of local business over massive, faceless companies, and thereby reduce CO_2 emissions, is going to be a sure-fire hit. Look at what is becoming unacceptable in our society – such as airfreight – and make sure your business does not encourage any activities that are fast destroying the biosphere. Remember: this is an issue of your children's future as well as your own.

There are other ethical issues that you might consider during the planning and execution of your new media strategy. Merely persuading people to buy more and more unnecessary goods is slightly irresponsible. Of course it is fun to have new clothes and a new car every year, if you can afford it. But the modern world has sent our industry in some strange directions. Every shopping mall is trying to push more and more unnecessary plastics, fabrics and leather into our possession. As we get richer we get more and more greedy. As the economist EF Schumacher observed in his brilliant 1973 book, *Small is Beautiful*, where is the society that says, 'Stop, we have enough'? There is none.

Very large parts of the world have had their traditional lifestyles destroyed by colonialism. Now these damaged cultures need our help to recover from the exploitative practices of giant corporations. So how can the damage to the environment be reduced? When considering ways forward for your business, think less about goods and more about services. Learning can be more fun than buying trainers. Style comes more from how someone behaves than what they wear. These are facts but also commercial opportunities, and they play well into the hands of emerging business.

Twenty years ago discrimination against women was rife in

business. Now it is beginning to disappear. Over the next twenty years, the corrosive culture of 'earn more, buy more' may be replaced by a more mature and sustainable form of progress. Only smaller, local businesses can possibly have the local intelligence necessary to inject diversity and strength back into community.

Over time, people may come to see the best investment for the future as a new qualification rather than a new car. They may prefer to spend more time walking and talking than working 60 hours a week to buy a few designer clothes. Maybe people will learn to share their drill, or lawnmower, or car with neighbours. They need not do this because they have become nicer: it just makes sense to avoid unnecessary expenditure. Sharing things is a huge commercial opportunity that innovative smaller companies will exploit. If you share more, you can buy less. If you buy less, you need less money. And that means you can work shorter hours. Freedom is a strong and powerful pitch.

New media channels such as interactive TV and 'M'-commerce are ideally suited to helping people share existing goods rather than buy new ones. Auction sites such as eBay.com are the tip of a vast iceberg. Following on from consideration of community assets, six factors converge to provide the new market opportunity:

1 oversupply of unnecessary goods
2 huge surpluses of durable goods
3 people working excessive hours to buy yet more
4 an environmental crisis that demands we manufacture less
5 electronic media that can facilitate the optimum use of existing resources
6 an entrepreneurial culture, facilitated by new media, that can grasp the opportunity.

Innovative smaller businesses can claim moral authority and huge, local intelligence. They can save us from bloated, homogenising chains. In this new century, if your business is not part of the solution, customers will assume you are part of the problem. Let big business do their worst, and you do your best. People know the difference between right and wrong. Kings and queens with great estates have given way to more civilised forms of government. Giant companies with thousands of branches, in hundreds of countries, will fade for the same reason. They lack the complexity necessary to help us live life to the full. They cannot help but simplify and reduce, whereas our species loves to complicate and expand.

Big companies use TV advertising to drive smaller companies out of business. It is horrific but true that the average American citizen spends 3 hours 45 minutes each day watching TV. This has worked well for giant retailers. In 1950, Britain had 221,662 food shops; in 1997 we had 36,931. Almost 90 per cent of our shops were wiped out, and for what? Yes, the process simplified life, but did it improve it? So why not try something radical? Switch off the TV, and think about your area. After all, TV is fantasy, but your local area is where you actually live.

The box is dead. Long live smaller businesses. And let your business, and others like it, bring our society back off its knees.

Selected bibliography and references

Chapter 1
Henderson, Hazel, November 1999. *Beyond Globalization, Shaping a Sustainable Global Economy*, Kumarian Press
Lovelock, James, 1987. *Gaia – a new look at life on earth*, Oxford University Press

Chapter 2
Dickinson, Paul, 2000. *Beautiful Corporations, Financial Times*, Prentice Hall
Frank, Thomas, 1997. *The Conquest of Cool*, University of Chicago Press, Chicago
Fukuyama, Francis, 1992. *The End of History and the Last Man*, Hamilton, London
Korten, David, 1995. *When Corporations Rule the World*, Earthscan, London
Loewy, Raymond, 1988 (reissue). *Industrial Design*, Fourth Estate, London

Chapter 3
'Marketing Means Business for the CEO', Spring edition 2000, Bi-annual review of Marketing Practices from Chartered Institute of Marketing

Chapter 4
(Rufus Leonard), Summer 1998. *Managing Communications in New Media*

Chapter 6

Needham, Kevin (LinkMedia Communications Inc., http://
www.linkmedia.com), 'Building Trust: Building Business'

Pehrson, Marnie, 'Building Trust' (http://www.pwgroup.com)

Wood-Young, Thomas, 'Building Trust Results in Customer Loyalty',
(Wood Young Consulting, Colorado Springs, CO 80921)

Chapter 8

Asita Technologies (www.asitatechnologies.com)

Bahl, Romil, and Livingston, Jimmy, 'Tying the Knot' (Executive
Agenda III, 2, Q4 2000)

Brighton Media Centre (www.mediacentre.org)

diarymanager.com (www.diarymanager.com)

Rufus Leonard (www.rufusleonard.com)

Zott, Christoph, and Donlevy, Jon J, October 2000. 'Strategies For
Value Creation In E-Commerce: Best Practice In Europe', 3i
Venturelab

Chapter 9

Tybout, Alice M, and Sternthal, Brian, 1999. 'Connecting with consumers: the Four Ds of effective positioning' in *Mastering
Marketing, Financial Times*, Prentice Hall

Chapter 10

Olins, Wally, 1989. *Corporate identity: Making business strategy visible
through design*, Cambridge: Harvard Business School Press

Index

CENTRE FOR SMALL & MEDIUM SIZED ENTERPRISES

Warwick is one of a handful of European business schools that have won a truly global reputation. Its high standards of both teaching and research are regularly confirmed by independent ratings and assessments.

The Centre for Small & Medium Sized Enterprises (CSME) is one of the school's major research centres. We have been working with people starting a business, or already running one, since 1985. The Centre also helps established companies to reignite the entrepreneurial flame that is essential for any modern business.

We don't tell entrepreneurs what to do – just help them be more aware and better informed of the opportunities and pitfalls of running a growing small enterprise.

Much of our practical knowledge is gleaned from the experience of individuals who themselves have been there and done it. These kinds of business coaches rarely commit their observations to paper, but in this Virgin/Warwick series they have captured in print their passion and their knowledge. It's a new kind of business publishing that addresses the constantly evolving challenge of business today.

For more information about Warwick Business School (courses, owner networks and other support to entrepreneurs, managers and new enterprises), please contact:

Centre for Small & Medium Sized Enterprises
Warwick Business School
University of Warwick
Coventry CV4 7AL
UK
Tel: +44 (0) 2476 523741 (CSME); or 524306 (WBS)
Fax: +44 (0) 2476 523747 (CSME); or 523719 (WBS)
Email: enquiries@wbs.warwick.ac.uk
And visit the Virgin/CSME pages via:
www.wbs.warwick.ac.uk

Also available in the Virgin Business Guides series:

LITTLE e, BIG COMMERCE
HOW TO MAKE A PROFIT ONLINE

Timothy Cumming

Now that the first wave of dotcom mania has passed, the right way to run a website is becoming clearer. If you haven't taken the e-Commerce plunge yet, or if you want to get more out of your website, we'll introduce you to the world of e-customers, e-competitors and e-suppliers, taking you through the practical steps of getting and staying online. You'll find out what e-Commerce really is and how to do it properly – and, above all, profitably – so you can make money instead of draining your resources. With the expert advice in this book, you can stay ahead of this fast-moving game.

ISBN 0 7535 0542 8

KICK-START YOUR BUSINESS
100 DAYS TO A LEANER, FITTER ORGANISATION

Robert Craven

Feel your business could do with a tune-up, but are too busy running it to sort out the problems? With the fast, proven techniques in this book, you can transform your workplace into a powerhouse. The case studies, worksheets and practical exercises will help you to take the pain out of business planning, increase your profitability and keep your customers. You'll find out how to identify your company's strengths and weaknesses and assess its potential, and learn the secret obsessions of all successful entrepreneurs.

ISBN 0 7535 0532 0

Also available in the Virgin Business Guides series:

THE BEST-LAID BUSINESS PLANS
HOW TO WRITE THEM, HOW TO PITCH THEM

Paul Barrow

Planning is not just for start-ups – it's the key to successful business development and growth for every company, new or old. But once a business is up and running it's all too easy to concentrate only on day-to-day operations. If you're launching new products and services, taking on more people, relocating to bigger premises, buying a business or selling one, you'll do it better if you plan it. This book shows you how to present the right plan for the right audience – so you stand a better chance of getting what you need. The sound practical advice, case studies and exercises in this book will help you through the planning process and ensure that yours are indeed the best-laid plans.

ISBN 0 7535 0537 1

Forthcoming titles in the Virgin Business Guides series:

THE BOTTOM LINE
BUSINESS FINANCE: YOUR QUESTIONS ANSWERED

Paul Barrow

'My business is growing and profitable but how come it is always so short of cash?', 'Is it true that I could need nearly half my annual turnover just to fund my debtors and stock – and why?' In this book the answers to these and other frequently asked questions are provided in short, easy to read and understandable sections. These are also followed by case studies, giving short insights into what other businesses have done and why it worked for them. The book covers topics such as: understanding financial statements, financial analysis and control, break even analysis, profit improvement, securing the right type of funding, and buying and selling a business. For those running or managing a business, *The Bottom Line* is invaluable in helping you find the answers you need to today's questions and gain the level of understanding of finance that you need to avoid problems in the future.

ISBN 0 7535 0569 X